The Future

D1378699

Verso Futures

The law of the innermost form of the essay is heresy.
– Theodor Adorno

Verso Futures is a series of essay-length philosophical and political interventions by both emerging and established writers and thinkers from around the world. Each title in the series addresses the outer limits of political and social possibility.

Also available in Verso Futures:

The Future

Marc Augé

Translated by
John Howe

VERSO

London • New York

This English-language edition first published by Verso 2014
Translation © John Howe 2014
First published as *Futuro*
© Bollati Boringhieri 2012

All rights reserved

The moral rights of the author have been asserted

1 3 5 7 9 10 8 6 4 2

Verso
UK: 6 Meard Street, London W1F 0EG
US: 20 Jay Street, Suite 1010, Brooklyn, NY 11201
www.versobooks.com

Verso is the imprint of New Left Books

ISBN-13: 978-1-78168-566-2 (PB)
ISBN-13: 978-1-78168-567-9 (HB)
eISBN-13: 978-1-78168-568-6 (US)
eISBN-13: 978-1-78168-718-5 (UK)

British Library Cataloguing in Publication Data
A catalogue record for this book is available from the British Library

Library of Congress Cataloging-in-Publication Data

Augé, Marc.
 [Futuro. English]
 The future / Marc Augé ; translated by John Howe.
  pages cm
 ISBN 978-1-78168-566-2 (pbk. : alk. paper) – ISBN 978-1-78168-567-9
(hardback : alk. paper)
 1. Ethnology–Philosophy. 2. Future in popular culture. 3. Civilization,
Modern–1950–Philosophy. 4. Future in literature. 5. Flaubert, Gustave,
1821–1880. Madame Bovary. I. Title.
 GN345.A92213 2014
 303.49–dc23
                                  2014025614

Typeset in Sabon by Hewer Text UK Ltd, Edinburgh, Scotland
Printed in the US by Maple Press

Contents

Chapter 1
Individual Future and Collective Future

The subject of this book is the future.

Not the future in the sense of 'what is to come'. That is a somewhat myopic concept that we project without much thought onto ill-defined groups ('What future are *we* shaping for our children?') when we talk, again without much thought, of *our* presumed inadequacies ('*We* are accountable for the future of *our* children') or *our* hopes ('Science is the future').

Not that future, but the future as a time of conjunction, the most concrete time of conjunction if it is true that the present is always ungraspable, ever retreating with the ceaseless passage of time; and that the past is always obsolete, irremediably finalized or forgotten. The future as life in the process of being lived individually.

That future is essentially obvious, while we are in perpetual doubt over 'what is to come'. What it boils down to is current events which give a content to the future by occurring. On that basis it can arouse every hope and every fear. There are societies in which occurrences, as pure contingency, are experienced as unbearable: they are interpreted, to slot them into the structure, and thus make them into a normal, expected expression of the order of things. Misfortune in general and illness in particular are investigated with a view to identifying the individuals responsible for them, but also to reaffirm the existence of an immutable norm: that is why their anthropologies (if this term is understood to mean a coherent body of representations assembled over time and transmitted from generation to generation) already include definitions of the individual, of the body, of consanguinity and of the collection of interpretative tools that make it possible, when the occasion arises, to explain apparent disturbances as indirect expressions of the norm. Taken together, these elements comprise a set of instructions which ethnologists analyse piece by piece in chapters covering, for example, kinship, the notion of the individual or beliefs in magic and sorcery. But the 'persecutory' conception of misfortune corresponding to this type of interpretation (when someone falls ill or dies, someone else must necessarily be the cause), while most spectacularly expressed in those human groups in which the individual is closely, substantively and structurally integrated with the collective, is only one of the modalities through which human societies in general try to account for events by fitting them into a logical and chronological succession. The past is never wholly occluded either on the individual or the collective level.

The future, even when it concerns the individual, always has a social dimension: it depends on others. Any episode seen as a 'stage' in an individual's life (an examination, a competition, a job, a marriage) depends to a large extent on people other than himself and fixes him more firmly in the web of collective obligations. It is sometimes said that the individual 'constructs' his future, but others participate in that enterprise which is primarily a manifestation of social life. Inversely, people speak these days of the social 'exclusion' of those who apparently have no 'future', who complain and protest because their assignation to a miserable and continuing present is experienced as the equivalent of a death sentence.

So, both senses of the 'future' are expressions of the essential solidarity between the individual and society. An absolutely solitary individual is unimaginable, just as one sort of future without the other would be unbearable. But inversely, to subordinate an individual to collective standards and his future life to what befalls the group smacks of totalitarianism. The radiant future once promised to the popular masses was a contradictory and impossible idea, in that it implied the stopping of time and thus the disappearance of the future – and of the individual with it. Basically it is the same with the future as it is with happiness. The object of democracy is not to ensure the happiness of all, but to create the conditions for it as a possibility for each individual by eliminating the most obvious sources of unhappiness. An acceptable future for all would be one in which everyone could manage their own time and give meaning to the future by individualizing their personal futures.

The real problems with democratic life today stem from the fact that technological innovations exploited by financial capitalism have replaced yesterday's myths in the definition of happiness for all, and are promoting an ideology of the present, an ideology of the future *now*, which in turn paralyses all thought about the future.

So what is proposed here is a dual approach, a dual study. We will start by examining the two main modalities of relation to the future observed in the diversity of human societies: the one which makes the future a successor to the past, the schematic one; and the other which makes it a birth, an inauguration. Both have acquired institutional and cultural forms of expression. We will also consider what is becoming of these two modalities in the contemporary period. Singular or collective, individual or social, purely temporal or historical (all these aspects remaining indissociable for the time being), the future is today taking on a new dimension and displaying several faces. It arouses multiple fears, but also – because man as a symbolic creature cannot live without some awareness of others and of the future – recurrent expectations, hopes and utopias. It is the acceleration of these 'mood swings' and the accentuation of this bipolar character, common to collective mentalities and individual sensibilities, that characterize henceforth our relation to the future.

At the hinge-point of these two moments we will try, using the example of Flaubert and *Madame Bovary*, to examine the notion of creation and, more specifically, to what extent a work of literature can anticipate the future or inaugurate it.

Chapter 2
Outlining the Plot, Expounding the Intrigue

The links between life and art are so close that it is sometimes hard to know in which direction borrowed words are tending. Originally, an 'intrigue' or 'plot' meant a complicated, embarrassing or nefarious scheme; for that reason the terms have been used about love affairs and political affairs, while also spreading to the theatre.

We are interested in the plot of a play or film because it stages a problem whose solution we expect: we are expecting the plot to be *resolved*. So long as it is not (and in principle it is not resolved until the end), we live in a 'suspended' time, the *suspense* found at its most intense in detective films and novels. This expectation arouses a specific pleasure derived from a particular relation to time: the real time spent reading or watching the spectacle, and the fictional time of the plot itself. The dénouement or resolution may contain surprises and, while awaiting it, the reader or spectator is not usually able to anticipate the retrospective reading that the detective hero will provide at the end. Our pleasure is born firstly of a pure form of expectation; knowing that all will become clear, we long to hear the end of the story in whose rhythm we are caught up, but we also know that our pleasure depends on that desire which depends on our expectation; we appreciate the author's skill at 'making the pleasure last'.

The paradox of the detective or police thriller is that it is usually written in the past tense, about events anterior to the present of the investigation aiming to elucidate them, but nevertheless affords the reader or spectator a vivid awareness of the immediate future. Fundamentally, in fact, this is the paradox of any literary or cinematic work: while offering the reader or spectator a few moments of anticipation and desire, in reality it already exists in completed form as a book, film or DVD. Everything is settled from the start. Some impatient individuals break the spell and destroy the illusion by reading the last few pages first, or arriving in the cinema during the closing minutes of the film (this used to be a common experience in the days of continuous programming; it is rarer today, but video and the change from public to private screenings make any chronological manipulation possible), thus condemning themselves to seeing the adventure as already written into inevitability via an inexorable narrative leading to an unavoidable end. Expectation of the unavoidable has a lure of its own (one well understood by tragic poets), but it proceeds from a retrospective reading of history which denies the existence of the future as an opening onto the radically new.

More subtly than such voracious, over-curious types, we may sometimes find ourselves taking pleasure in rereading a novel whose ending we have not entirely forgotten, or seeing again an old movie, thriller or other, still faintly present in our memory. In those cases our pleasure, setting aside anything to do with beauty of expression or aesthetic feeling, undoubtedly stems from the rare opportunity to combine memory and expectation. In cinema, we rediscover the faces, landscapes and events absolutely identical to the ones we had seen in the past (with a certainty that memory alone normally refuses), but we are also caught up anew in the rhythm of the narrative and the expectation of the dénouement, even when we remember it. Of course – and this applies even more to rereading a book – we come across forgotten details, or aspects that passed unnoticed the first time; we don't necessarily have the same gaze. So the experience is one that also speaks of ourselves, which is what gives it its special intensity: the private upsurge of a future which had been put behind us.

Three further comments on the word 'plot' (in French, *intrigue*). It has clearly pejorative connotations when applied to the covert manoeuvres we suppose to exist in social and political life: plotters are people who care only to achieve their aims, especially by bringing their 'connections' into play; they follow a skewed, falsified and untruthful (but social) conception of life. The adjectival form 'intriguing' on the other hand has a much more positive sense, referring not to the idea of mystery, which suggests something unknowable, but to curiousness in its dual aspects, passive and active: we describe as 'curious' something that awakens curiosity. An intriguing phenomenon excites both the curiosity of the inquisitive individual and his desire to take a closer look. In all cases, the intrigue is only resolved by deconstructing a complex tangle of interpersonal relations, *social* relations: for good or ill, the intrigue – the plot – brings into play the relations that comprise social life.

In the theatre they are represented, in a novel they are

described, and in a thriller we try to discover them in their raw reality behind the mask that conceals them.

In any event, working up a plot establishes a dual relation with reality. It poses a question which has to be answered, and in that sense impinges on the future. But once set up, the plot requires to be resolved: in other words, the solution to the enigma is initially oriented towards the past, even if it claims to liberate the future. The assumption is that the key to the future always depends on the past.

The ritual logic evoked at the beginning of this book proceeds from the layout of a plot. Whatever its ultimate purpose (to explain a misfortune, to master a vicissitude or ensure an orderly transition), it achieves it through a systematic review of the past. Allow me to return briefly to the conceptions of misfortune that underlie accusations of 'witchcraft'. The idea that any misfortune or illness springs, directly or indirectly, from the wishes of another person (hence belonging to what medical anthropology calls social aetiology) is traditionally very widespread in, for example, African lineages; when someone dies, a number of procedures are undertaken to determine the identity of the culprit who is, quite literally, put on trial. Explanatory templates pre-exist the enquiry. They can cover lineage as well as matrimonial alliances, paternal kinship and maternal kinship; in some societies it is claimed, for example, that attacks through witchcraft take place more easily inside a lineage (patri- or matrilineage), but it is also accepted that an attack by the father, in a matrilinear society, or by the maternal uncle in a patrilinear society, remains a possibility; still other scenarios can be envisaged in reference to witchcraft (exchange of crimes within a magicians' society itself presented as the maleficent double of the age-class system) or outside that frame of reference (a god of voodoo type may get annoyed with someone who neglects his shrine). All of these theoretically envisageable scenarios have two complementary characteristics in common: rejection of contingency (the diagnostic procedure aims to operate a return to the intellectual, symbolic and social order) and a perpetual referral to the past as the only possible source of meaning. I was astonished, during my first stay in Côte d'Ivoire, to note that everyday life in the village, swarming with rumours concerning the sick and the dead, resembled a sort of perpetual police investigation.

Ritual, as we know, addresses two types of event: specific events which arise at moments when they are not necessarily expected, but also recurrent events, like the changing seasons; in the latter case ritual is undertaken not to banish the event but to ensure that it takes place. Once again, people want to act on the future, but a future conceived and desired as identical to the past. The wish for such regularity, most important in regions of the world where any climatic upset can have catastrophic results, is nothing new to us. Even as a child I can remember hearing people say that there were no proper seasons any more, and we have all noticed the anguished perplexity aroused today by the prospect of global warming. Human groups need temporal references just as much as spatial ones, and the theme of seasons is used metaphorically in a wide variety of contexts: sport, politics, literature, education. The year is punctuated by re-entries or 'terms' which give it a rhythm and channel our vision of the immediate future. In France the expression 'social re-entry' (*rentrée sociale*) is even used to designate the protest campaigns which, after the summer holidays, often accompany worker demands and the resumption of labour. Working up a plot is an aspect of that setting of things to rights. Observation of meteorology can give seasonal change – when it comes late, for example – a dramatic character in some parts of the world. And under the present system, we see how the media insist on dramatizing the most expected and recurrent episodes of political life, or announcing with startling emphasis the most trivial rivalries in the new sporting calendar. It seems that more fundamentally, the meteorological metaphor is a substitute for ritual activity aimed at mastery of the future; independently of its stated purpose and official objectives, it contributes to the symbolic ordering of the world by trying to banish the fears aroused by perception of the inexorable passage of time.

The prophets I met in Africa called themselves prophets, a title they borrowed from the Bible, and like the biblical prophets they contented themselves with short-term predictions, on the scale of individual lives. Harris, the first of them in Côte d'Ivoire, announced in 1913 that within seven years blacks would be on a par with whites. During the 1960s and '70s, following decolonization, his successors saw the figure of President Houphouët-Boigny, the country's first post-independence leader, as symbolizing the promise of rapid development. Meanwhile they devoted themselves, as healers, to the care of individual maladies which they interpreted in terms of the old logic: they did not deny the existence of the sorcerers they claimed to be battling, but in healing people, or believing that they did, they thought (not without an element of contradiction) they were illustrating the advent of the new era.

The colonial influx was incommensurate with the

phenomena traditionally managed by ritual activity. An event par excellence, an advent, it was the sign and proof of a radical change on which it was imperative to have a position. It was 'intriguing' in itself, surprising, and it led to a questioning both of the past which had made it possible and of the future it heralded and even prefigured.

Prophets, in Côte d'Ivoire and elsewhere in Africa, especially in the Congo and South Africa, added a personal stamp to the traditional procedures for deciphering intrigues: they too wanted to be both sign and herald, they would be the first manifestation of the new times they announced, and their own material and social success would stand as evidence of this. Many failed, and those who made a name for themselves did so by creating a place, a conspicuous setting for their activity, building stone or concrete churches and establishing more or less close relations with the political authorities, both before and after independence. Adherence to the person of the prophet gave access to the new world: that was the essence of their message.

Was it so different from the message of our own politicians? Working out a plot is not restricted to lineage-based societies, and it constitutes an unavoidable stage in apprehension of the future. Reinterpreting the past to imagine the future, in a short-term way, is what all politicians do. The economic conjuncture, we are told for example, is the cause of our current difficulties. Certain sacrifices are needed to avoid an even more catastrophic situation. But through a policy of rigour we will restore our finances to health, encourage investment, restart the economic machine and boost employment. Give or take the odd detail, this discourse is always the same; we hear it all the time. It bores us with its monotony, it sounds increasingly perfunctory, and sometimes we would at least like to hear it interpreted by another voice. That is what we call 'alternation' in politics. The very word assumes a basic continuity – in musical language, a sort of basso continuo – with superficial, purely formal variations. The presupposition that subtends the relative passivity of the citizens and electors, although they may deny it, is that the 'situation', the existing state of affairs, is impassable, immovable. It is what it is, and what it is comes from the past, the solidified past that dictates the words used, whether in specialized jargon or the demotic, to say everything that can be said about the future. Outside the extremist parties, from which only incantatory propositions are heard, evocation of the past almost always precedes invocation of the future, conceived broadly as a simple extension of the past.

Nevertheless, along with lassitude and discouragement, we still find passion and desire in democratic political life; as if, against the evidence of daily disillusionment, a majority – variable and fluctuating no doubt – was stubbornly set on taking part and expressing themselves by voting, taking industrial action, going on marches. 'I know, but all the same': denial of doubt is not willingly abandoned. If it is true that ambivalence is defined by the coexistence of two affirmations (I am this *and* that) and ambiguity by two denials (I am *neither* this *nor* that), in facing the political future we show ourselves as more ambiguous than ambivalent; we are neither optimistic nor pessimistic, but reveal ourselves to be attuned in advance to any plotline that might offer a way past that double denial.

Ambiguity is the armature of a dialectical conception of reality and history which lays heavy emphasis on contradiction, and which is thus responsible for the importance we ascribe to the role of the past in every domain. That role is undeniable, and it would be absurd and dangerous to ignore it either in the life of groups or of individuals. But to use it as the explanation for everything, to make it the sole actor, is to risk ignoring in our relation to time all that falls outside history, or more exactly evades historical determination: intuition, creation, commencement, volition, encounters.

We should however note, in this connection, that working out the plot can be approached from two points of view: in relation to the past during which the plot took shape, and in relation to the future during which it will be resolved. In the logic of the police thriller, the two viewpoints are confounded: the past has to be examined to find the solution, and the various vicissitudes that may arise during the investigation (other murders, false trails, assorted suspects) find their definitive explanation there. The police thriller is not written in the past, or the present, or the future, it conjugates all three. It is infused with ambiguity. In an adventure novel, by contrast, the plotline is open; and it may, to tell the truth, gradually take on shape and complexity in the course of incidents and encounters. *Robinson Crusoe* begins with the shipwreck which the hero survives. The question is, will he continue to survive? Crusoe has a past, but he is obliged to shed it for the time being and live in the present, while scanning the horizon over which there may come the future which will enable him to retrieve his past. The adventure novel is written in the present and in the future and in the past. It is infused with ambivalence.

By applying the term 'grand narratives' to the myths of modernity, Lyotard, in *La Condition postmoderne*, underlined the narrative dimension of the utopias and ideologies born in the twentieth century. He said that these visions were immediately distinct from myths in the traditional sense, in two respects: they spoke of mankind in general, of humanity, not of a particular group like earlier cosmogonies and cosmologies, and their bearing was on the future, not on the origin. Hence these visions of the future inspired the programmes of progressive movements, especially in their Marxist version. Marxism featured actors, the different actors of the class struggle, and suggested a plot outline whose ineluctable development would be driven and fuelled by the emergence of latent contradictions within the relations of production. That scenario, that working up of narrative and plotline, attempts to combine history with commitment, historical inevitability with the obligation to struggle. A character in Malraux's *La Condition humaine* complains about it on his deathbed: why must one sacrifice one's life to the struggle, if victory is guaranteed in any case by the dialectical advance of history? Thus the history of the twentieth century may also be that of the failure of these grand narratives, not only because of the failure of communism (at least in its Western version), but even more because of the murderous totalitarian monstrosities they ultimately produced. Let us note here for the moment that the revolution brought about by the myths of modernity, influenced by Darwinism, favoured recourse to the past in deciphering the present. This only became problematic when, going on from that, it aspired to infer the future.

The psychoanalytical grand narrative is as ambitious as the Marxist one, and aims to be no less universalist. Borrowed from Greek mythology, the central character of the scenario – an indefinitely reproducible scenario applicable, in theory, to the whole diversity of human beings – appears exclusively on the individual stage, removed from historical context. However, although the unconscious has no history, it has a past, one which encumbers the individual in myriad ways and offers for interpretation his slips as well as his dreams, his phobias as well as his desires and, in general, his relations with others, with life and death. The psychoanalytical narrative has impregnated a lot of human activities, especially the creative arts, but I would note that, in its integral or integralist variants, which refer the individual back to his past and his personal 'mythic nightmare' while inviting him to produce his own interpretive narrative, it is to be found today only in a few Latin countries. However, we live in a talkative era, one in which the public display of opinions, reactions, declarations and diverse 'comings out' has reached a level seldom seen in the past. The need to tell one's story, to make a narrative from one's personal life, is common to all; indeed, it is only the expression of the symbolic dimension of the individual, who needs the presence of others and of words to really exist. The exchange of news in the street, the bar or the office is an essential manifestation of the social dimension of existence; but this type of exchange remains mostly vague, limited to the ongoing banalities of everyday life by way of predictable propositions, and does not aspire to reveal the inner personality of the speakers. The pleasure that results has to do with its superficial aspect and its redundancy.

On the other hand, television and the internet are full of new-style confessions touching on every aspect of private life, which all share two characteristics: they are public, and they suggest that revelation of the past can alone render the future liveable. Reality TV goes further by purporting to create live on air, experimentally as it were, a plotline in the form of a game in which the immediate past and the near future collide and telescope together. What is going on is not so much a Christian confession as the 'psychologization' of minds via a soft reference to psychoanalysis. After just about any drama of modern life – road crash, air disaster, fire, flood, armed lunatic running amok – teams of trained psychological 'counsellors' are rushed to the scene (in Europe, not in Somalia or Syria). Filters and euphemisms to protect the feelings of 'vulnerable individuals' are multiplying by the week. To protect them from what, exactly? From the recent past. If the exhibitionists of private life have a guaranteed audience, and assistance to the relatives and friends of accident victims is actually necessary, it is not because the hard knocks of history have made the individual psyche weaker or more dependent on others, but rather because when the past disappears or collapses the psyche is confronted with its solitude in the blank image of a terrifying future.

When the past disappears, meaning is erased: such at least is the lesson preached by most religions and philosophies, one that has been orchestrated for more than a century with particular force, in continuity with Christianity and the ideology of original sin, by Marxism and psychoanalysis.

Chapter 3
Inauguration

We need first to re-examine the category of the 'new', to look at novelty itself, this concept having been somewhat besmirched by the fashion business and journalism.

'Deep into the unknown to find what is *new*!' exclaims Baudelaire in *Les Fleurs du mal*. But really it was an interpellation of death: 'O Death, old captain, the time has come! Let's weigh anchor!' And a reference to an ancient opposition: 'Hell or Heaven, what matter?' The remarkable thing about this call to the unknown and the 'new' is not so much that the poet is addressing death, but that in so doing he should be constrained to use the old notions of Hell and Heaven. It is difficult to evacuate words that continue to clutter the memory, even when their content has become inexact. They continue to exist, still pregnant with the images associated with them, faint and wispy though these may be.

Any reflection on the new is thus dependent on an examination of freedom. To return for a moment to our earlier thoughts on the logic of lineage-based societies, we will readily admit that, to the extent that it imprisons individuals in an intellectually constrictive totality that predates any initiative, it severely limits the possibility that anything radically new may occur, along with any pretension to individual freedom. But the question also arises in the case of science, if it is valid to wonder whether the notion of freedom is compatible with that of truth. Sartre illustrates this well in *Situations I*, in connection with Cartesian liberty. He starts by admitting that the test of freedom is different in the domains of action or creation and in those of discovery and comprehension: 'A Richelieu, a Vincent de Paul or a Corneille would, had they been metaphysicians, have had certain things to tell us about freedom because they grasped it by one end, at a moment when it manifested itself by an absolute event, by the appearance of something new, whether poem or institution, in a world that neither asked for it nor rejected it.' Then he identifies and analyses the two definitions of freedom present in Descartes's thought. The first gives full rein to autonomy and volition, for freedom allows a choice between accepting or rejecting ideas conceived by the intellect (in which case nothing is ever final and the future is never predictable). The second conception, closer to Spinoza's, is more restrictive, freedom as the capacity to recognize the truth and embrace it willingly: here, the clarity which arises in the intellect governs volition. Sartre ends by suggesting that Descartes only lays out his full conception of liberty in his writing on divine freedom: it "is known without proof and merely by our experience of it".

Does freedom really ensure the possibility of the new in history, and is art really a manifestation of that possibility? Sartre is convinced of it, and criticizes psychoanalysis essentially for not being dialectical, in other words for being reductionist, for favouring the past over the future. We know for example that Flaubert, 'the family idiot', backward, coming late to language, 'seized language because it was withheld from him', and to gain his father's approval. But why reduce a work to the past from which it proceeds and against which it is a reaction? '*Madame Bovary* is not only a succession of compensations, but also a positive object, a certain relation of communication with each of us.' Any flight is also a project, and 'Flaubert by fleeing from himself paints himself.' In the category of project there is something that cannot be reduced to the sum of predeterminations that weigh on it.

I would add that an optimistic conception of the future may not be the sole product of hypotheses on the possibility of the new. Like that of freedom, the idea of novelty only has meaning in relation to human existence. When we think of the future, a number of mental attitudes are put in place corresponding to different points of view. We are situated in relation to the future as mortal individuals, affective individuals with personal attachments, as seekers or as militants: many other positions are conceivable, and each person may occupy several simultaneously. We are also situated, and this is important, as beings already engaged with time, young or old: expectation, hope, impatience, desire and fear, none are the same at different ages in life.

It is true that different conceptions of the future are then at work, not opposing continuity and novelty, but rather the new as succession, flowering, completion and the new as rupture, inauguration, beginning. The ethnologist is at home with this distinction. Not because he assigns to the groups that constitute his traditional object of study – lineage-based, tribal societies, primitive by comparison with industrial societies – a necessarily stagnant or repetitive conception of history. But because, on the contrary, he knows from repeated personal observation the extent to which the ritual activities used to manage public and private affairs are aimed at producing and bringing into existence the possibility of a commencement.

It is important here to be as precise as possible in defining our terms. For a start, we should not confuse events or 'news' with history. The reason why we have been tempted to speak of such societies as being 'without history' is that we paid too much attention to the procedures they use to reduce the contingent aspect of events, to make them expressions of the social structure. The lagoon-dwelling groups with whom I worked in the 1960s and '70s maintained the memory of the migrations which had brought them to the banks of the Ébrié lagoon. My Alladian informants could recall and repeat the circumstances surrounding the foundation of the various present-day implantations, the role played by the trade in sea salt with countries further inland, and later by trade with European ships, notably in the second half of the nineteenth century with the boom in palm-oil exports. The social changes brought about by these historical ruptures had not escaped their attention, and they made a lucid analysis of the matrimonial strategies or the massive purchases of slaves that had enabled the big coastal traders, while preserving the essence of the matrilineal structure, to assemble a labour force wholly subject to their authority by modifying traditional social relations from top to bottom. History had made them, and they had to a large degree made their history; at the very least the chiefs of the biggest lineages had done so, consciously and systematically. Domestic slavery had long been considered a form of encouraged and controlled immigration. But that practice was in no way contradictory with the ritual practices undertaken to manage events conceived as an expression of the structure, indeed quite the contrary.

There are two dimensions to ritual when it is carried out properly: it has its rules; from this angle, it is rooted in the past; it is executed with rigorous fidelity to the rite established by the ancestors; at the same time it is focused on the future, and the emotion attached to its celebration is born of the feeling that it has succeeded in bringing something into being, that it has produced a *beginning*. Similarly, the ceremonies to welcome and introduce new captives of either sex into the Alladian matrilineages in the nineteenth century (I was given detailed descriptions) told them first and foremost that they must forget their origins, and staged, with a richness and ceremonial scale appropriate to the importance of the moment, a new birth. In this example, extreme (because it marks a radical social transformation), the ritual is expressed in its essential form, which aims to create the feeling of a beginning. Beginning, rather than novelty, is the specific purpose of ritual.

Just as ritual is essentially a birth, so every birth calls conversely for a ritual. Each human birth is the object of ritual procedures in which it is possible to read the watermarks of the twin, contradictory obsessions which govern social life: the obsession with meaning, which harks back to the past, and the obsession with freedom, which looks to the future. Every birth opens a future, eminently fragile in countries with high infant mortality rates. To continue with African examples, I would recall that in West Africa, the newborn's body was examined, closely scrutinized, for anything that could pass for the mark of an ancestor: a partial heredity that, once recognized, could lodge his identity in the past. The rules of naming responded to the same wish. For centuries it has been the same in Europe, where, without necessarily being associated with any theory of partial return, Christian names are still often passed on from generation to generation, at least for boys. Otherwise, a 'primitive' conception of heredity held sway and it was seen as obviously suspect if a boy or girl did not resemble the father, albeit subtly. The 'legitimacy' of a birth was a form of 'life insurance', the support of the past organized socially for the adventure of an individual life. Godparents, in the Christian tradition, added a supplementary support to the contributions of descent, symbolized by the giving of another Christian name.

Interestingly, some children these days carry the first names of cinema or television stars. Thus, Kevin was a very fashionable first name in France a few years ago. This phenomenon obviously reflects a weakening of kinship structures as a principle of meaning. It departs from (social) meaning and leans towards (individual) freedom. But there too, the freedom is only for the parents. Real freedom would consist in an individual being able to choose his own name. The anonymity that cloaks some online exchanges and the widespread use of pseudonyms no doubt give the 'Web acrobat' a more or less playful sense of impunity, but they also foster the illusory and poten-tially dangerous conviction of circulating in a separate world in which the need for meaning (sought through 'social media') and the need for freedom (by creating avatars) can be reconciled. We all know of film and show-biz celebrities who have changed their name for career reasons, the equivalent in their eyes of starting a new life, with risks and opportunities that – in principle – no longer depend on the family past. Conversely, of course, we also know of small dynasties, acting families that pass the torch from generation to generation, as if to combine individual talent and family heredity, a principle of freedom and a principle of meaning.

A beginning is the purpose of ritual. A beginning is not a repetition. People sometimes say: 'Look, it's starting all over again', meaning that there's no change. The important element in that is 'starting'. Starting again is living through a new beginning, a birth. When Molière's Don Juan says that he is susceptible to 'nascent inclinations', he is placing himself, beyond any calculation or strategy, in the truth of the moment called 'falling in love'. Repetition only arises at the time of 'disinfatuation', when the scenario, in effect very hackneyed, emerges in the everyday truth of its recurrent dénouement. But in the original moment itself, all that could be perceived was the poetry proper to every beginning, as far as could be from cliché and repetition. Don Juan is insatiable and tireless in pursuing the emotional turmoil of a first spark constantly repeated. After that he loses interest, incapable of living a love story to the end. The Proustian narrator is made of the same stuff, even if his position is symmetrically opposite Don Juan's: he declares that he is no longer capable of falling in love and does not want to, because since all love must end he would experience its beginning as a sort of death.

In all episodes of individual and collective life, in the amorous as in the political life, we are aware of signs of attrition which we may attribute to betrayals by others, but which from a distance appear to us – even more seriously perhaps – as irremediably linked to the simple action of time, to a form of historical erosion or quasi-biological ageing which generates enormous nostalgia in return. 1789, the Commune, 1936, the Liberation, May '68, the green paradise of childhood loves or the Time of Cherries are celebrated and sung long after they have lost their inaugural force and completed their backwards ascent into myth. In modern life at least, myths are born when rituals die and lose their creative power. Does this mean that the beginning never outlives the moment, and that disappointment must always be the far-reaching shadow of ritual?

Fortunately, things are not so simple. Of course we are mortal and everything in us is mortal. Even in the most successful lives, no willpower can prevent love from subsiding into affection, passion into politeness or anger into resignation. It is in the sphere of relationships, or social meaning, that our fragility can be seen; with time, not only do old connections weaken or dissolve, because of forgetfulness or death, but new ones are lacking. If all goes well, however, an 'ageing' person, threatened with irremediable solitude, may find the strength to redefine their relationship with younger generations by accepting that age may be the beginning of another adventure. All can be understood by all; all can speak to all; if not, the likelihood is of symbolic exclusion, living death, the arrest of time.

Art, culture and education have a fundamental role to play here, and that is why ageing is primarily a political question. Material ease and intellectual capital are statistically associated with a longer and more interesting life. And it is precisely the faculty to evoke the future, near or remote, that determines how interesting life is. Without that, awareness of having to die one day would obliterate any desire to live. We think of Baudelaire once again, and his poem 'Guiding Lights' in *Les Fleurs du mal* on the great painters like Leonardo da Vinci, Rembrandt or Goya whose names punctuate the history of art:

> a cry repeated by a thousand messengers . . .
> . . . the beacon flares on a thousand citadels!

The poem is admirable in that it is addressed to the share of generic humanity we all carry within, expressed by the use of the pronoun and possessive adjective of the first person plural, *we, our*:

> This, O Lord, is the best evidence
> that we can offer of our dignity,
> this sob that swells from age to age and dies
> out on the shore of Your eternity!

What Baudelaire's poem does not say, although it is illustrated in each of the stanzas he devotes to the original universe of each master painter, is that the call or appeal he describes is both similar and different each time: each time a new beginning, both echo and extension.

Art offers to one and all the opportunity to live through a commencement. What belongs to the principle of all creation also belongs to that of all perception and all reception (I avoid use of the economic term 'consumption'): to read a book, listen to music or look at a painting is to appropriate them, and in that sense, recreate them; authors are well aware of this: what they want is to encounter an audience, and no encounter is one-way only. An encounter, contrary to heredity, heritage and destiny, is the ordeal of otherness (the reason why the word signifies empathy as well as confrontation) and an opening-up of time, adventure and freedom.

That is surely why mythologies have tried to occupy the terrain in advance: the crossroads, an ideal setting for encounters, is marked out, symbolized, protected, to prevent it from becoming the scene of 'bad encounters'. Greek mythology, with Oedipus and Laius, made it the setting for the fulfilment of the Delphic oracle's prophecy, and psychoanalytical mythology the symbol of the original curse held to oppress every human individual.

Literary and artistic creation thus defines the problem area in the individual and collective adventure. Absolute beginning and opportunity for extraordinary encounters, or supreme illusion of humanity alienated from its original destiny? The tension between meaning and freedom is here at its peak. It is expressed, in the most banal and trivial way imaginable, in our relations with the so-called minor arts, which are also the most ordinary and the most widely shared: popular music, for example. The trite refrain of a tune heard a thousand times which a random busker in the subway has to belt out a bit flat on an accordion to screw a few coppers out of his captive audience? Or the sudden bolt of instantaneous emotion, ephemeral but very real, which can pierce us on hearing one bar of a song we once liked but that now, far from awakening the past, liberates the faint, fleeting, tenacious suggestion that, whatever our age, whatever our problems, *something* is still possible; that life can be conjugated in the future tense?

We need that intuition, and the need is itself a sign: a sign of life in whose absence man, a symbolic animal, cuts short or outpaces the biological clock by means of suicide.

A relation to the other, even in the form of memory, promise or project, forms part of him; he reanimates it incessantly in his everyday behaviour and seeks its traces or proofs in the surrounding world and its events, including such adulterated forms as the 'personalization of political life' or a sporting competition. We have to be able to think of time as a plot outline but at the same time, in complementary fashion, as an inauguration. That is why ritual still attracts us today, why we sometimes feel the need for it and seek it out. For the absence of ritual characterizes the society of transparency and the eternal present in which we now live.

The beauty of a painting, a poem or a piece of music, when we are sensitive to it, is never the same twice. Each repeat experience arouses a new emotion, so that knowing from experience what is going to happen, we first engage as far as possible in some small private ritual in order to prepare ourselves: small adjustments of various sorts, depending on place and circumstance, to ensure the requisite calm, silence and composure. The role of performing artists both underlines and masks this dimension. It underlines it, because the fact that dramatic or musical writing supports different interpretations reveals the abundance of virtualities that different voices, movements and bodies will succeed in actualizing. It risks masking it, nevertheless, to the extent that we are tempted to believe that only the conductor's direction, the interpretations of soloists and instrumentalists, the originality of the stage director and actors or the subtle voice control of the poetry reciter are at issue here, when really, in the secrecy of our internal lives, as the only interpreters of the work we are hearing or reading again, we often experience deep within us the inaugural force. It is natural that the force should be multiplied in public performances by different performers, since they reinforce the ritual aspect and render the social dimension of the art more palpable.

The social dimension, which here takes the form of the encounter, is carried to its highest pitch of excitement in the great gatherings of young people around the more fashionable musical groups. We should note – a glance at the television will confirm it – that, however demonstrative the body language may be in these circumstances (raised arms waved in time with the music), it remains classical: the public *sings along* with the lyrics and snatches of melody it remembers, and that embody something it recognizes. The singing along is not a repetition, but a moment of communion when everything starts over, when the meaning of the words matters less than the unshakable perception of a movement of belonging which has no object but itself. As if Aristotelian catharsis were being replaced with the immediate evidence of a pure leap of the soul, boosted by the double presence of the one on stage on whom all eyes are fastened, and the many in the crowd who gain, from such a palpable coming together, the certainty that they exist.

Chapter 4
Self-Denial or Creation: Flaubert

The tension between meaning and freedom which concerns us here is exemplified by the paradox of Flaubert. Alienated (as we would say, in a language that was not his) from their reading, from their dreams and from ambitions which did not really belong to them, his characters are primarily expressions of an era. Nevertheless he worked hard to write them into existence, as if nothing was more important than giving shape to the disillusion that not only robbed them of any poetic vision of the future, but endowed the more lucid among them with a resolutely pessimistic view of the past itself. At the end of *L'Éducation sentimentale*, Frédéric Moreau, the survivor of amorous passion, and his old friend Deslauriers, the survivor of political ambition, exchange youthful memories and in particular recall a seedy visit to the town brothel. 'That was where we had the best of it,' Frédéric Moreau concludes.

Despite the autobiographical elements found in romantic fiction, and the reciprocal effects that can make an author seem to resemble his character, the fact remains that one is the creation of the other and that the principle of the novel is not reliably to be found in the resulting narration, or in the personalities of the invented characters, often mouthpieces for their creator, but more often (and this is the essence of the novel) in the illustrations, or examples, of his proposition which it contains. This dissociation is nowhere as marked as it is in *Madame Bovary*.

Madame Bovary first appeared just over 150 years ago, in 1856, in *La Revue de Paris*. On rereading *Madame Bovary* today, one experiences a feeling of familiarity, but also of surprise. Obviously the familiarity comes from the numerous readings of the novel itself, and of commentaries on it, that one has had occasion to make over the years; but this is a 'strange familiarity', to use Freud's expression. It does not come down to a phenomenon of habit, culture or memory. It is immediate, it has something in it of the actual, and it is that actuality that provokes surprise and a hint of unease.

Flaubert, it is often said, invented the modern novel by focusing on everyday ordinariness and the petty-bourgeois characters who hitherto had played only secondary roles in the romantic novel, forming part of the background. In his work we find no evocations of high society, as we do in Balzac and Stendhal, nor of the path of social ascent followed, or dreamed of, by some of their heroes. Flaubert is the painter of immobility and stray impulses, depicting a milieu so heavily oppressive that any attempt to escape from it is necessarily the product of illusion. In that sense he could be defined as the first post-revolutionary novelist, the first to distance himself both from Enlightenment language and the effusions of romanticism. No one can deny that he thus broke with all his predecessors, opened a new perspective and invented a language. We still need to understand, however, why this old rupture seems so close to us today. A rereading of *Madame Bovary* may help.

Madame Bovary is a banal story whose very banality made it a sensation: two adulteries and a suicide, the story of a woman, unsatisfied in every sense, who after seeking intense sensations in literature, religious imagery and amorous transgression, can only escape from her surroundings in death. This dismal story gives Flaubert the opportunity to attack everything he detests: public morality, religious morality, good manners. It is hardly surprising that he faced trial under the Second Empire for denigrating those recognized and official values. But you do not have to read much of Flaubert to notice that he has no particular sympathy for the victims of those values, or for those of his characters who claim to oppose them in word or deed. *Madame Bovary* is, then, a novel as paradoxical as *L'Éducation sentimentale* would be twelve years later: not only is there no 'positive' hero with whom the reader might somewhat identify, but the narrative is not really centred on a single character. Apart from that, it begins with a brief account of the childhood and youth of Charles Bovary and ends with an even briefer account of his death. To be strictly accurate, the last word is given to the pharmacist, Monsieur Homais, that impenitent chatterer, symbol of the happy stupidity protected by public opinion: we learn in the last line of the novel that he has 'just received the Legion of Honour'.

Of course, Emma Bovary is the novel's main 'heroine'; she frees herself to such effect that in the view of many she embodies the condition of middle-class women and of an 'inauthentic' relation to life and history, 'Bovarism', defined as a retreat into the imagination from an unsatisfied existence. But Flaubert's offering is not limited to the life of a woman, or to the depiction of a social milieu or an era. The reason why *Madame Bovary* remains a literary milestone of the first importance, and why philosophers never stop referring to it and examining it, is undoubtedly that it is, in Flaubert's own words, a novel 'about nothing'. In what follows I shall pause over this expression, which occupies Sartre's attention in *L'Idiot de la famille*, and seems to me to express both Flaubert's ambivalence and his ambition.

The 'nothing' which Flaubert tries to describe is also 'everything', everything there is to be said about anything at all, everything one has 'gone through'. Flaubert in effect has 'gone through everything', the exhilaration of travel, the thrills of love and the illusions of politics. People sometimes say, to mark a very stark alternative, 'it's all or nothing'. In Flaubert's vision this is not an alternative but a synonym. Everything that is described, in the end, is that 'nothing'. But that 'nothing' is not an empty void; it adopts forms, it manifests itself, and that is why it is possible, through writing, to hunt it down, close in on it and show it for what it is: the insignificant, always and already there, which repeats itself, which persists, only to say whatever we make it say, indifferently, whether chatter or silence, project or memory, being or appearing.

Flaubert starts this pursuit of nothingness by staging effects of repetition. One generation repeats another, for example. At the beginning of the novel, Charles Bovary's childhood is described, and in the process the evanescent figure of Madame Bovary *mère*, who seems to foreshadow her second daughter-in-law but will nonetheless be the object of her hatred and jealousy: 'Living in such isolation, she shifted onto this childish head all her scattered and broken vanities. She dreamed of high office, she already saw him, tall, handsome, talented, established, an engineer, or a magistrate.' Also repeated is what we commonly call destiny, which is much influenced by social, family and economic position. The first wife of Charles Bovary (a decent fellow who might well be called an involuntary serial killer) was a bailiff's widow, chosen by his mother for the double reason of respectability and solvency. She could hardly survive for long the revelation of her financial ruin and the shame of poverty: 'She had been telling lies, the little lady had! . . . A week later, as she was hanging out the washing in the yard, she had a seizure and spat some blood, and next day, as Charles turned his back to draw the curtains, she said: "Oh! My God!" heaved a sigh and passed out. She was dead! How astonishing!' The last repetition concerns the disappointment that inevitably follows, often very quickly, sometimes more slowly and insidiously, after the slightest leap of imagination, the slightest attempt to expand life beyond the daily routine; marriage, of course, but adultery as well. Unstable emotions and precarious relationships are ordeals from which people emerge destroyed or indifferent. In Flaubert's vision, women are more exposed to the cruelties of disappointment than men, who are more easily comforted by material well-being or petty-bourgeois vanity. They too endure repetition, but suffer less or not at all, even extracting from their amorous relations a sort of fatuous narcissistic satisfaction, verging on lassitude or indifference.

Perhaps indifference is, along with repetition, the word that best explains the nature of that 'nothingness' which fascinates Flaubert and haunts his writing. The subject is so faintly defined in *Madame Bovary* that the reader is often unsure who is speaking or who is feeling. The novel begins with the evocation of a 'we' that refers to no one, if not, on first appearance, a narrator who seems to have been a schoolmate of Charles Bovary ('We were at prep, when the Head came in, followed by a new boy not in uniform . . . We had a custom, on coming back into the class-room, of throwing our caps on the ground, to leave our hands free . . . We saw him working conscientiously'). But this anonymous 'we' soon disappears; the witness withdraws and gives place to the author, or more accurately to the objective and impersonal description of the words and deeds of the characters. But the characters are themselves so undifferentiated that they are often evoked, even when named in the narrative, through the impersonal pronoun '*on*', which seems almost to assimilate them into a shapeless organic mass just capable of obeying conditioned or programmed reflexes. 'One', 'you', 'they', people in general, could mean all those who are looking on and who may eventually utter calumnies: 'Then, upon reflection, he decided that his mistress was beginning to behave strangely, and perhaps people were right in wanting to disentangle him from her.' It could also mean a small group of people doing the same thing at the same time: 'Two and a half hours now, they had been at the table . . . Once he had the priest's umbrella in his free hand, off they went.' There was the '*on*' of the social machine ('they were coming out of church') and the quasi-fusional '*on*' of shared perception and sensation, as during the first horseback ride of Emma and Rodolphe ('It was early in October . . . there appeared in the distance the roofs of Yonville'). Lastly, '*on*' is the impersonal subject in which all the others participate, who stands in for the author and describes what the protagonists of the narrative are supposed to see and hear ('There were people leaning out of every window . . . and you heard, erupting suddenly from behind, the drawn-out bellowing of a cow'). '*On*' is thus alternately identity without subject and subject without identity: that nothing and that everything with which the novel deals.

The fact is that sensation, an immediate and fleeting sensation or one that unleashes extremes of dizzy folly, lies at the heart of what Flaubert describes. But sensation, however intense, is both fragile and confused. It seems to invite disappointment, because it is at its strongest when still in the form of a presentiment: 'Future blessings, like tropical shores, project onto the immensity preceding them their inborn softnesses, a perfumed breeze, and one grows drowsy in that intoxication without a moment's thought for the horizon one doesn't even notice.' Sensuality combines the charms of reminiscence with the magic spells of expectation. Old sensations and faces from the past can invade the present in an instant. In an early encounter between Emma and Rodolphe: 'It was in this yellow coach that Léon had, so many times, come back to her; and along that very road that he had gone away for ever! She thought she saw him over the way, at his window, then it was all a blur, clouds went past; it felt as if she was still turning in the waltz, under the bright chandeliers, on the Viscount's arm, as if Léon were not far away, was going to come . . . and yet all this time she could smell Rodolphe's hair beside her. The sweetness of this sensation went down deep into her past desires'. Between the presentiment and the confusion, distance is abolished. Distance brings misfortune to Emma Bovary because, sooner or later, she always watches it re-establish itself between herself and those she believed she loved, or wanted to love. But the confusion is even worse. If one recalls the other, if the images of Léon and Rodolphe are superimposed, it is because one is worth the same as the other. When time is not creative, past and future are abolished together: nothing passes, nothing happens. Emma has placed herself definitively under the sign of repetition, incapable of living through a true beginning.

Confusion can also reconcile. Charles Bovary, mad with pain and jealousy after Emma's death, is oddly comforted by his encounter with Rodolphe, her former lover: 'Charles went into a dream as he looked at the face she had loved. He felt as if he was seeing something of her. It was miraculous. He so wanted to have been this other man.' But confusion is dangerous; it activates a principle of generalized equivalence that, by way of the enjoyment of pain, demolishes the distinction between life and death. Charles Bovary goes to sit on his garden bench and dies without being aware of it amid the voluptuous splendour of a summer day: 'the vine leaves threw their shadows over the gravel, jasmine perfumed the air, the sky was blue, cantharides beetles were droning round the flowering lilies, and Charles was choking like an adolescent from the vague amorous yearnings that swelled up in his aching heart . . . At seven o'clock, little Berthe, who had not seen him that afternoon, came to fetch him in for dinner . . . thinking he was only playing, she gave him a gentle push. He fell to the ground. He was dead.'

Jacques Rancière has referred in several articles to Flaubert's 'democratic' vision of the real. For the Flaubert who wrote *Madame Bovary*, the description of some vegetation in the landscape is as important as that of an episode in the characters' lives. Others have spoken in this connection of Flaubert's 'pantheism'. It must be said that description, in his work, is so detailed and at the same time so vivid that it has evocative value. Flaubert's Normandy exists, not only in the particulars of its sociological reality (markets, roads, farms, towns, dialects) but through the force of its landscapes, its sounds and smells. It simply exists in itself. No link is postulated between the characters and their milieu, whereas with Balzac a description is always the equivalent of an explanation. Flaubert himself often said that Emma Bovary could have lived elsewhere, in another village, another country. So are we to think that he is interested only in the psychology of a frustrated woman? That he tried deliberately to produce the prototype portrait of a woman confronting, with consistent ill-luck, the empty seductions of the modern world, that he is deep down the first novelist to depart from local colour and come to grips with what is not yet a globalized world, but already a society of stereotypes, in which soothing images of prefabricated well-being collide with the violence and boorishness of social and economic reality? That what he was really describing is more the truth of a moment than a place?

It is possible, in fact, to retain that hypothesis, and at the same time point out that there is an ethnological or anthropological tendency in Flaubert, since it is around a singular (albeit fictional) experience that he has drawn his prototype portrait. The author of *Madame Bovary* has the sensibility of an ethnologist divided between participation and distance. We know that in the Orient he liked to dress and live in the indigenous manner. But what travel really taught him was the experience of distance and, through that, something of himself: loyal and disloyal, he dreamed of the Orient when he was in France and of going home to France when he was abroad. Today he might be called unstable. The merit of that instability was that it enabled him to look at society with an unforgiving gaze. He detested above all things its stupidity and hypocrisy. He lacked the spirit of a revolutionary, however (and was to maul with equal severity those with revolutionary pretensions in *L'Éducation sentimentale*). Moreover he was misogynistic, while quite aware (as his correspondence shows) of the degradation imposed on women by the society he loathed. Emma's dual exemplarity in Flaubert's mind is beyond doubt: she speaks of women but also of the society which shapes them.

Flaubert's pessimism goes further (if it really is only pessimism, and not nihilism). The principle of equivalence and indifference which he sets literally to work applies to beings and things, but also to time (projects and memories carried off in the same tempest) and to feelings. His absolute materialism is unleavened by any hint of social or political illusion. Nor does he believe in any future, literal or abstract. For these reasons he remains resistant to the sociological and philosophical deconstructions to which he is constantly subjected. He has one weakness however, which is also his strength: writing, the ambition to write down that nothing which is the truth of everything. Why does writing seem to fall outside, to distinguish itself from, nothingness?

At this point opinions may diverge.

Some will say that writing is the ultimate illusion, even an illusion twice over, in that it aspires to analyse a phenomenon of which it is just a symptom. My rereading of *Madame Bovary* gives me a very different feeling.

The fact that Emma should be such a contemporary

and troubling figure today, so that we may even feel we understand her better than her contemporaries did, certainly owes something to Flaubert's writing. Through its very economy, it proves able to capture the smallest material detail, the most fleeting hesitation of speech or tremor of the spirit, but also to grasp, in the harmonics and resonances of the era, an effect of stereoscopy whose echoes will only become perceptible later and further on. As Michel Leiris has pointed out, you have to be totally of your time to be able to survive it. Being contemporary means concentrating on those things in the present that sketch something of the future. Briefly, it is only from a distance, starting with the observation that he is still *present*, that we can judge the *pertinence* of an author to his period and find something personally relevant in what he has managed to distil from the formless chaos of his reality.

In *Le Ruban autour du cou d'Olympia*, Leiris considered the parallel question of how to locate the specific features belonging to a given period. And, using Manet as an example, he suggested that a detail in a painting (in this case the modest black ribbon and the paste jewel attached to it) constituted such an indication of contemporaneity. He also saw it as an encouragement to the ageing author, who starts to wonder whether he is still 'in the loop' as everything around him becomes increasingly incomprehensible: he can, after all, still hope that he has left a few signs for those who will come after him, signs unnoticed at first, but which may be regarded in retrospect as characteristic of his time. Contemporaneity is not to be reduced to passing events and is conjugated in the future perfect.

The future perfect is the ultimate trace of optimism

required by creators. Flaubert 'will have been' the one who in creating Emma Bovary foreshadowed the illusions, alienations and tragedies to come; perhaps he was aware, in identifying himself with his heroine, of reaching far beyond, doubly so: for although it cannot have been comforting to imagine, based on scrutiny of the present, the imminent, looming mediocrities, the idea that those who would come to know it later might find a prophetic echo in the cold, passionate ferocity of a nineteenth-century novel would have given Flaubert a prospective empathy with his future readers, his ideal readers. I think again of Baudelaire and the opening of *Les Fleurs du mal*: 'Hypocrite reader – my alias – my twin!' I have no doubt that Flaubert was conscious of writing partly for those who would understand, much later, the extent to which he had been contemporary with their time as well as his own; this helps explain the paradox of a man who believed in nothing, except in writing (and therefore in the future after all).

But despite his claim, which history has recorded, that 'Madame Bovary is myself', Flaubert is Flaubert and Emma Bovary is Emma Bovary. The heroes of novels rapidly escape from their creators; they have an existence of their own that overflows the authors' imagination. Very soon they cease to belong exclusively to the author. Readers appropriate them by identifying with them, and there are perhaps as many heroes as there are readers.

The epic hero was sometimes a demigod. Demigods illustrate the passage from chaos to plotline, from myth to narrative, the gradual advance out of the 'mythic nightmare' through literature posited by Benjamin, and the gradual substitution of a human world for the world of the gods analysed by such writers as Paul Vernant and

Cornelius Castoriadis, with reference to tragedy in particular. At the end of the journey, man discovers that he is alone. Then appears the face of the real hero, one who believes neither in paradise nor in historical progress, but who still consents to carry on living . . . or who dies for a lost cause: a Camus or Malraux hero. But Flaubert stood at the opposite pole to such godless mysticism. His heroes are characters without heroic traits. Apart from Emma, really, because she has anticipated the conclusion which her successors in heroism, a century later, will not dare to reach: that in the face of meaninglessness there is nothing but death. Emma is the heroine of taking action, doing something, the anti-hero par excellence; but the anti-hero is an extreme form of hero, whereas Frédéric Moreau, by contrast, is simply a non-hero.

Renunciation of a personal future through suicide does not necessarily signal renunciation of the world's future, 'what is to come'. Heroic death, in general, is meant to prove something: the martyr is betting on the world's long-term future even as he renounces his own immediate one. That gamble on the world's future, though, is not devoid of more personal elements. Like the writer's future, it is conjugated in the future perfect; it aspires to transform a life into a destiny. There's nothing of that ultimate gesture, that supreme grandiloquence, with Emma: her suicide, a pure renunciation of life, remains a private matter stripped of all illusion and any pretension to exemplarity. Emma's existence and future are only literary. That could be what Flaubert meant by saying 'Emma Bovary is myself'. He is the real hero. He believes in nothing, but writes all the same.

We are more or less consciously aware, in our consumer society, of the dissolution of reality into appearance being operated by the media, of the forms of solitude that come with the development of communications and the principle of equivalence or indifference which seems to be taking over everyday history and information. Affective life is increasingly modelled on stereotypes broadcast across the whole planet. Intellectual life is increasingly influenced by codes of the most conventional correctness. Caution, correctness, respect: these general and undifferentiated watchwords exercise a tyranny over every moment, commonplaces disguised as moral stereotypes that do little to conceal the disarray, rage or anxiety of the individual.

Idiotic superstitions, irrational tyrannies and religious mania are striving, not without success, to disseminate themselves in the name of freedom, and we do not even know who is responsible for this uncontrollable drift. We fear everything. We are afraid of our own shadows. We wring our hands and ask forgiveness for the sins of our forebears. We are becoming used to the idea or image of a world without history or future, a world that has arrived, a finished world whose space is closing in on itself for good. What ironic or punitive barbs, what thunderclaps might be inspired in the author of the *Dictionnaire des idées reçues*, if he could return among us and hear the claptrap being churned out all day long by two-bit pundits of every kind, in tones of smug certainty, pedantic expertise or crazed proselytism, and endlessly parroted by a captive public? If Flaubert's heroine still touches us – more than ever – it is because she prefigured these new insanities. And besides, the middle-class environment in which she moved appears, in all its complacent banality, more familiar to today's reader than the tormented romantic aristocrats of Tolstoy's novels. In this sense, although twenty years her senior, Emma Bovary is closer to us than Anna Karenina, that other towering and tragic figure of female modernity.

To what doomed aberrations might Emma Bovary resort nowadays, to escape the unbearable mediocrity of her condition? I imagine her sitting dreamily in front of her TV or computer screen. Is she going to let herself be seduced through a dating site by some marketing or human resources executive? Will she try to meet him for a giant cocktail before dinner, or on a cruise ship all expenses paid? Will she be tempted to follow the example of those young celebrity-obsessed women she sees on television, singing or talking about themselves with a studied passion and license that sometimes bring a blush even to the cheek of a seasoned old producer? Will her intransigent character expose her to the risk of those murderous disappointments in love from which, after a few times, recovery is possible only on the cinema screen? Will she die of an overdose, or be pushed under a subway train by a lunatic one evening in rush hour? Unless she jumps in front of it herself . . . but in blaming someone else she can be robbed of her very death.

Emma Bovary speaks to us of the impossibility of flight, the unachievable dream, dying feelings that fade into indifference, the cupidity of some and the weakness of others, and the individual who is everything and nothing. She suggests to us that in a time of ubiquity, an eternal present of generalized fictional imagery, Bovarism is no longer only the fate of neurotic provincial women: it transcends the frontiers of gender and pathology. Or to be more precise, it helps us understand that women have always embodied the human condition at its most tragic. Man's grandeur and misery: Pascal made a wager on it, but what did his sister think? What did Chateaubriand's sister think, and Claudel's? By the grace of male self-importance and egocentricity, the condition of women can seem the worst form of human misery. 'Woman is man's future,' the poet wrote. Aragon was more right than he realized. Behind his promise one nevertheless detects a warning. Consumption of tranquillizers and anti-depressants is rising in the so-called developed countries. People commit suicide at work. We keep blundering into glass partitions, into our own ghostly, scrambled reflections. Behind its curtain-walls and TV screens, the planet is changing into an aquarium. In this enclosed world, simultaneously opaque and transparent, this world from which you do not escape, it is tempting to think that the lucidity without hope of Bovarism could be the only way out, the only justifiable madness in this world of lunatics.

Before trying to live or to survive, we have to face that hypothesis, sweep aside the pretences of the obvious, identify the threat and ponder whether or not to resist it. Must we really plumb the depths of despair because we are disillusioned, renounce ourselves and others, our own future along with the world's? Or should we give up the illusion of despair, the parade of vainglorious suffering, and accept the mediocrity of the everyday with non-heroic wisdom, face a bleak future without promise? Such are the terms in which Bovarism continues to interrogate us.

The planetary crisis now under way has a deep dimension that transcends economics. It is not simply financial. It is not simply political or social, and it is not of recent origin. The year 2000 passed, accompanied by overblown fears, but it still is not out of the question that future historians may speak of a Hundred-Year Crisis in connection with the period we entered quite some time ago now.

Moreover, the way it is perceived forms an integral part of the crisis. Its direct victims – more broadly, those who suffer it because they are hardly in a position to do otherwise – are suddenly becoming aware that something has stopped working, something has shifted without their knowledge. Crisis, crisis of conscience and dawning awareness succeed and boost one another, but it is impossible to make sense of them in terms of cause and effect.

Death or 'nothing': is that the only choice?

Chapter 5
New Fears

We have yet to draw all the conclusions from the change of scale now affecting life on the planet.

This change is fundamentally economic and driven by technological development (technological innovations generate new consumer goods which then bring about new forms of organization of labour). Capitalism has succeeded in creating a market that extends across the whole earth. Big companies are escaping from the logic of national interests. Financial logic is imposing its own law on states. And this dominion has suddenly become so glaring that it is unarguable, beyond appeal, give or take the clamour from the protest demos that accompany it without changing anything. The class struggle has taken place, and has been lost by the working class: the triumphant International is the capitalist one. Of course, the system still undergoes crises, but no one would now dare claim that they signal contradictions gravid with progress.

The planet is being urbanized, equipped and reorganized, and in the process the urban landscape is being radically transformed. The grandiose downtown architecture of US cities and European commercial districts symbolizes worldwide, in the most direct way, the power of the businesses which look down on the daytime world from those glittering towers of mirror-glass, and at night fill half the sky with the light pouring from the ever-illuminated offices within. The protesters, when they manage to make themselves heard, are themselves imprisoned in the world of images created by the prodigious expansion of the media and electronic communications. In just a few decades our most familiar surroundings have been transformed. The categories of sensation, perception and imagination have been disrupted by technological innovations and the power of the industrial apparatus projecting them.

The body is being kitted out, drugged and doped with increasing efficiency. Soon we will be working to improve its performances with nanotechnologies, by inserting microprocessors in a glorious form of electro-neurological graft. Those 'bionic' men or women we remember from '70s and '80s TV series, able like creatures from tales by Perrault or Grimm to see further, hear more acutely and run with seven-league strides, are on the way to becoming reality. The paradox of that triumphant body, though, is that it is no longer anyone's body: it escapes the control of its putative owner; it is the captive of the techniques or substances that propel it beyond any normal performance, much as an individual sentenced to wear an electronic tag is the prisoner of his magic ankle bracelet. When the seductive charms of fiction penetrate reality they arouse first astonishment, then misgiving, and finally a dread of man's being dispossessed by his own inventions. Fear of the sorcerer's apprentice is ever-present, especially as technologies to produce high-performance, invulnerable bodies tend to fall primarily into the military orbit. At the very moment when fighting machines are beginning to replace soldiers (think of drones), the human body aspires to machine-like invulnerability and power. It is surely over-fanciful to imagine robots one day being transformed into men, but much less so to imagine the reverse and worry that men may be becoming robots. There are historical precedents dating from well before these technological inputs.

Traditionally, the anthropologist studied social relations in groups small enough to enable him to work alone; he attempted to understand those social relations by examining them in their context. Today the context is always a world context, even in the depths of Amazonia or the middle of the Sahara. As I recalled in *La Vie en double*, the notion of non-place applies from the start to all the constituents of the global context in which any local study is now contained. The spread of empirical non-places gives us an idea of what tomorrow's world will be like, and corresponds for individuals as for groups to a change of scale that modifies the definition of the context (always planetary in the final analysis). The instruments and spaces of communication form part of the context but also of the relations, and in the end their development may have the effect of casting doubt on the distinction between the two. Ethnologists of the future trying to analyse the workings of social media will surely have trouble separating the type of relations arising in them from the environment of which they are part and which they help to define.

The change is political. Rising powers, 'emergent' countries are in the news, along with their demands for proper representation in the international bodies. But two potentially contradictory languages can be discerned in this context.

The old language is connected with nations as such, and conceives their future competition in terms of the preceding centuries. A few indices – growth rate, trade balance, debt level – supply the data to measure their relative positions in a planetary race, seen as analogous to the one that opposed the European nations in those earlier centuries. Formerly colonized or subjected nations 'join the club', undertake in their turn to 'sit at the top table', and put so much enthusiasm into it that they are soon going to overtake the front runners. The UN and other international bodies are comfortable with this language in discussing (for example) which countries will be the next members of the Security Council.

But another language has made its appearance, more transnational than international. It serves to talk about local conflicts. Local, because a 'world' war between great powers has become unthinkable since the collapse of the Soviet Union and China's conversion to the market economy. Wars, in the old sense of the word, are today restricted to small countries and are essentially civil wars or frontier conflicts. Many factors may thus be involved, complicating the search for solutions, but it is reasonable to predict that these types of confrontation will eventually be subject to the right of intervention or arbitration (and possibly of sanctions) by bodies like the International Court of Justice.

This does not mean that the planet will be more peaceful, or that the great powers will play no further part in unleashing violence, or that new forms of warfare are not appearing on the scene (economic warfare, industrial espionage, cyber-attacks, terrorism); but the modalities are different and those responsible less easy to identify. Fear is changing its aspect, too. No one in Europe fears a classic type of conflict these days. Fear is becoming vague, diffuse; every new outrage compounds it.

Dating the first appearance of words and tracking their diffusion would be an eminently sociological exercise, in the most precise sense. In the domain that concerns us here, two types of word are involved.

In institutional vocabulary the UN, dubbed a 'contraption' or 'thingy' (*machin*) by General de Gaulle, has become real to everyone; people may complain about wavering by Brussels, IMF policies, actions by NATO or OPEC decisions, but they know from reading the papers and watching the news that these labels designate regional or transnational entities whose initiatives affect us directly.

In conceptual vocabulary, the word 'governance' (meaning roughly 'art of management') is a neologism seized upon, some years ago now, by the politicians in charge of the globalized world; it implies in effect that everything is a matter of competence and good management. We seem to have left the domain of dreams and revolutions for good. The concept of governance proclaims the end of history. It is the political watchword of a consumer and services society that should complete its encirclement of the whole planet before long; a society that would still care about its immediate future, but would no longer need to look further ahead.

The change is ecological and social.

The fears raised by globalization seen as the end of history are the counterpart of ecological fears. We are mistreating the planet and the ozone layer under the imperatives of development and growth. But apart from that, what is growing under this development logic is the gap between the richest of the rich and the poorest of the poor, between highly educated and illiterate. On top of this trend we can already see the outlines of a transnational planetary oligarchy and an unequal planetary society whose motor is to be consumption by the middle classes; an excluded mass (exclusion is another word which has had a new lease of life in recent years) will be parked on the sidelines, assisted and managed for what it's worth by specialized institutions which will, at best, support them a few cable lengths above the poverty threshold.

Fear of falling down on the excluded side is today very widespread, and feeds anxiety over the immediate future.

The change of scale is demographic.

The world population at the beginning of the twentieth century was more or less equal to that of China alone today. This demographic expansion is unequal between countries; most developed countries have declining fertility rates. It is easy to imagine – indeed they are often cited – the fears raised by that inequality. Two contrary panics strengthen each other mutually. Migration from countries where life becomes more difficult by the day is intensifying; migrants often risk their lives to get away. These movements of population arouse anxieties in their destination countries or regions, Europe of course, but also Africa, the Americas and Asia.

Migration is worrying because, among other reasons, it is one of the most visible manifestations of the changing planet and makes the artificial character of any narrowly local demand apparent to all. But identity is bound up with place and the fantasy of loss of the self is spreading, combining individual with collective representations when an unemployment situation, for example, is directly related to the presence of immigrants.

Behind these anxieties lies a deeper fear: that there may be too many of us on earth, too many for the earth to feed, too many not to exhaust vital resources.

The theme of resources running out is now explicit, and we are starting to deploy new technologies designed to palliate the effects. Demography – although this is not said openly – obviously lies at the heart of these ecological worries. And natural catastrophes whose effects are amplified here and there by human poverty and overcrowding, or by the presence of dangerous installations (for example nuclear power stations), seem capable of eliminating whole chunks of humanity. Under these conditions the prospect of a planet on which ten billion human beings will soon be jostling for a place can only redouble those explicit fears and anxieties.

The change of scale is aesthetic and cultural.

The Renaissance in the sixteenth century, first in Italy and then in France, passed through a return to Greek and Roman Antiquity, giving new life to the Christian tradition, but also had inputs from further afield (Americas, Africa, China) which Lévi-Strauss viewed as the source of European vitality and dynamism in that period. 'Here' in this connection was clearly Europe, 'elsewhere' the rest of the world. One sometimes wonders if things have really changed. The answer is that they have, because although there is still a centre of the world, it has been geared down and to some extent deterritorialized. The 'virtual metacity' cited by Paul Virilio consists both of the world's megalopolises (of which the most influential are situated mainly, but not exclusively, in the Americas, Japan, China and Europe) and of the exchange, communications and information networks that link them together. People today are more likely, in many contexts, to mention the names of towns rather than of the countries where they are located.

Big cities try to construct 'brand images' for themselves. They try to figure as often as possible in the list of awards given by the transnational institutions (designation as a World Heritage site, election as cultural capital of Europe, or less modestly and ephemerally, to be chosen as the venue for the Olympic Games or other world sporting championship). All these honours generally lead to the construction of emblematic and prestigious new buildings. The names of big architects are almost as well-known across the world as those of famous footballers. Architecture has acquired an altogether peculiar status. A threat to reduce the height of the tower being built by Nouvel in Manhattan by a few metres causes a press furore. A great Bordeaux vineyard adds prestige to its vintages by getting Mario Botta, architect of the cathedral at Evry, to design its new factory and storage building. When a new museum opens in Bilbao or Chicago crowds flock to see it, attracted less by its contents than by the edifice itself. The better-known architects are celebrated throughout the world, and even medium-sized towns try to inveigle one of their works onto their territory, gaining instant planetary status (and attracting tourists).

The big businesses which occupy the latest towers do so essentially to maintain their images. Image and brand are magical, fascinating concepts that sum up for many people everything it is possible to know about the world we live in. Such enterprises also claim to provide good working conditions for their staff. But those conditions are themselves often a matter of image. 'Open plan' offices are not really places of freedom allowing the gaze to rest on the distant horizon through immense plate-glass windows, but spaces in which everyone is imprisoned by the gaze of other people, since the business milieu tends to be rigorously hierarchical. This is apparent from the allocation of places in the 'open' space, and from the fact that the most senior staff have partitioned offices.

It is therefore important to distinguish between situations.

In a sense, everything circulates and everything is to be found everywhere. Thus in Brazil, small tribes thought to have disappeared have reappeared since the Brazilian government started a policy of land grants to socially constituted ethnic groups. Cross-bred, dispersed and isolated individuals came together and reinvented common laws and rituals, on the basis of memories and improvisation. In their ceremonies (much prized as spectacle by foreign tourists) they often use commercially available objects, usually of Asian origin: a clear case of the spread of material 'features' contributing to a cultural reinvention, a return to origins borrowing from outside sources. There is surely nothing truly unprecedented in this, and one imagines that groups and cults have always constituted themselves on the basis of this sort of 'cobbling'. What is new is the very remote location of some of the sources and the diversity of populations: it testifies to a new organization of the planet.

In the fields of art and design (which tend increasingly to blend and overlap), playing with forms and objects of remote origin does not result from the same constraints. It proceeds from a considered choice and acquires meaning in privileged circles aware of the immense possibilities offered theoretically and ideally by the exposure of the whole planet to everyone's gaze. It is the product of an inspired humanist eclecticism, opposed to cultural monopoly and ethnocentrism.

The problem for defenders of that sort of eclecticism, and for all artists these days, is the extreme flexibility of the global system, extraordinarily adept in dealing with all declarations of independence and all attempts at originality. Hardly have they been formulated than calls for pluralism, diversity, recomposition, redefinitions of criteria, or openness to other cultures are embraced, proclaimed, popularized and staged by the system, concretely, through the print and broadcast media, and by political and other bodies. Hence the feeling among the public at large – no doubt technically inaccurate, but sociologically revealing – that in art as in architecture, everything seems the same. The problem for art, in the broadest sense, has always been how to distance itself from the current state of society, which it nevertheless has to embody if it is to be understood by the men and women to whom it is addressed.

Art must express society (which today means the whole world), but it must do so purposely. It cannot simply be a passive expression, a mere aspect of the situation. It has to be expressive and reflexive to show us anything beyond what we see every day in the supermarket or on TV. The vocation of art is to be disturbing. The forms of contemporary art unsettle us by transforming familiar objects into objects of reflection; in doing so, far from sublimating reality, they *subvert* it. Their aims counteract the efforts deployed by the consumer society to persuade us that everything goes without saying, and the temptation immediately arises (encouraged by reassuring messages from the media) to reduce them to simple variations on what already exists, to mere redundancies.

The change of scale is physical and metaphysical.

Worries about the environment and the questions being asked on climate change are revealing with brutal suddenness to the common run of mortals the minuscule size of our planet in an infinite universe. 'The universe is a circle whose centre is everywhere and circumference nowhere', Pascal wrote. Science is producing a slightly more exact view of things: it seems there are billions of solar systems in our galaxy and billions of galaxies in the universe, if that word has a meaning. Of course these dimensions are beyond our imagination, and it is as well for our mental health that we do not generally try to wrestle daily with the mysteries of matter, black holes or the expansion of the universe. But insensibly, by a sort of osmosis, even the most ignorant can absorb the idea, all the more terrifying when it derives not from knowledge but from vague representations, that nothing is less to be taken for granted than nature. The earthquakes shaking commonplaces and common sense are far from harmless.

What is sometimes called the individualization of beliefs is therefore rather like an individual internalization of doubts and fears. The ancient cosmologies which wrapped human misery in a halo of meaning were the projections of societies themselves defined by their inscription in space and time. Now, at the very moment when new forms of mobility are appearing on earth, many of us are experiencing the more or less confused intimation of a perpetually expanding material universe of infinite size, which obviously far exceeds our ability to imagine it.

Chapter 6
Innovation

The idea of the model helps to give us a clearer conception of the difference between the action disciplines and the sciences. The models that emerged from nineteenth-century utopias had humanity as their object and were conceived by human brains. Once the model had been delineated it lost the character of a hypothesis – revisable by definition – and took on that of a guide to action. In other words, it lost any problematic dimension and came to be seen as a set of instructions for use, based on certainty: this was the difficulty faced, with belated and tragic common sense, by the hero of *La Condition humaine* as mentioned above.

Even when clearly separated from any ideological dimension, the social or human 'sciences' are not scientific in the same way as the so-called natural sciences, because they are focused on humanity itself: not the biological and material components of human beings, but human behaviour in its symbolic aspect, relations between the self and the self and between the self and others. Comparable measurement systems and, for example, the quantification of results play little or no part in them, and it is quite obvious that the discipline of economics falls into the social sciences category and is not one of the natural sciences, however 'hard' and formalized its investigative methods may be.

Since the social sciences were conceptualized by humans, they cannot exclude the reflexive dimension from their field of study. This is not to negate the tendential and ideal unity of all learning, nor to claim that the social sciences can only produce qualitative and relative results (quite the contrary); they are simply more exposed than the natural sciences (although those too are not completely exempt) to the risk of being taken over, or heavily influenced, by the forces whose interplay they study in the social field. Being part of that social field, they have more trouble than the natural sciences in adopting a viewpoint totally external to their object.

We are currently witnessing, with globalization and the extension of the capitalist market to the whole planet, a series of unprecedented convergences creating a radically new situation that the public only perceives in fragmentary fashion, owing to the speed with which it has appeared and the power of the language that presents it as self-evident, natural and indisputable. To characterize this situation briefly, I would say that we are no longer capable of addressing our relation to space and time – the basis of the symbolic activity that defines the essence of man and humanity – except by means of artefacts elaborated by industry and available on the market. It amounts to nothing less than a total disruption of any capacity human individuals may have to perceive their relation to themselves and others, a revolution apparently still in its first rumblings, but which could ultimately shift the parameters of what we still call human nature.

For the social sciences this situation represents a threat, an accomplishment and a challenge. A threat because the convergences just mentioned cast doubt on the role of the social sciences themselves, called upon more or less to become measuring instruments in the service of the technological transformations now under way. An accomplishment, to the extent that they succeed in turning their critical gaze on themselves and on everyday reality, as social anthropology sometimes did in colonial times, in order to take the true measure of the social phenomenon into which they are drawn. And a challenge on the scale of the stakes: are we hurtling at ever-increasing speed towards a post-human world, or will we manage to invent the principles of a new humanism?

Equally challenging is the fact that in real contemporary history, the diversity of local histories still plays an important role, and concrete history does not coincide totally with the scientific version, even though technological innovations give that impression in some parts of the world. The planet's diversity is still enormous. It is hardly acceptable merely to observe from a vast remove the spread of poverty, the brutalities committed by religion, the slide of politics into gangsterism or the grip of speculators on the world economy. In the past we used to call on 'emergency ethnography' to preserve a few traces, at least, of dying cultures. We face another sort of emergency action these days: to reintroduce the critical gaze in domains that seem natural to us, in that we are part of them without knowing how that came about; to use the weapons of analysis to question the unarguable or the unargued. We must not be scared by the changes taking place into rejoining the unending chorus of conservatives and reactionaries, but instead work to save the idea of progress by revitalizing the question of *ends*.

Fundamental research does not necessarily lead to inventions, not immediately at any rate, but every invention is the fruit of such research. As for innovation, a notion forged by Schumpeter in 1912, it is primarily defined as the introduction of invention into economic activity. Let us try then to leaf through the innovation file. Volume 7 of the review published by the Musée des Confluences in Lyon, entitled *Innovation*, is useful in that it presents a full table of the uses made of the word today.

Bruno Jacomy, executive director of the Musée des Confluences, specifies the definition of innovation and adds: 'Invention is the creative act through which an idea takes the form of a real object; innovation adds to that a social character, due to its diffusion through society in the form of a product' (*Innovation* 7, July 2011, p. 60).

So the notion is quite an old one, but it has never been so often brandished, celebrated and invoked as it is today. It is presented as the key concept of enterprises described specifically as 'innovative', and the word is part of the language and vocabulary of the private sector of economic activity; but this usage overflows into a range of other sectors, notably through the intermediary of the communications technologies largely developed by private companies. A number of themes are thus taking shape which at first sight seem familiar: commendation of diversity, participation, interdisciplinarity; linkage between the technical and social spheres, high status of research, continuous training, collaboration between academia and the worlds of business and administration, between research and industry, and so on. But we may wonder whether, in this new context, such themes perhaps function as a reduced metaphor for social life. More polemically, we may even doubt that it is still a metaphor and wonder whether we are in the presence of a vast scheme of substitution, changing the meanings of the terms 'research', 'diversity' and 'cooperation'; we may wonder if the world of business might not have substituted itself for the world proper.

Innovation, judging by the analyses of those attempting to define the concept and the realities that comprise it, recalls Marcel Mauss's 'total social fact', in that it concerns all aspects of society simultaneously and encompasses all of its actors.

To begin with, it is presented by the more attentive observers as a collective phenomenon resulting from interaction between different agents. The central idea is that the reactions and initiatives of users, especially in the field of IT, can make the system evolve by inventing and if necessary implementing uses not originally envisaged. This collective dimension of innovation originates historically in the observation that inventions quite often appear in several places simultaneously. Hubert Guillaud (*Innovation*, p. 50) cites in this connection two US experts on new technologies, Kevin Kelly and Steven Berlin Johnson, who have listed differential calculus, the electrical storage battery, the steam engine, the telephone and the radio among the inventions conceived at the same time by different individuals.

From this observation bearing on the relative internal coherence of different historical conjunctures we pass, a little hastily perhaps, to an optimistic view of the present period: an optimistic vision that manifestly corresponds to a form of commitment, in the social and political sense. Thus, Johnson undertakes to demonstrate that the cultural products despised by 'intellectual elites' – TV series, video games, reality shows – may have been a factor in the increase of average IQ over the last century. The term 'democratization' is employed by Eric von Hippel (*Democratizing Innovation*, MIT, 2005) to describe the role of users in the adaptation or modification of machines in current use. Even the pre-launch testing of Apple products on schoolchildren is held out as an example of this collaboration between users and conceptualizers.

The development of what (for some time now) we have called 'social media' is presented as having an eminent role within that 'collective dimension' of innovation, ever since instantaneous communication started to facilitate reactions, replies and exchanges. The so-called Research and Development sector of business, or R&D, is thus becoming the test site for the new model of innovation: cooperation. This can even extend to cooperation between competing firms, which otherwise maintain their autonomy, on some component or components of their output. This practice has been dubbed 'coopetition'. Another recent concept is that of 'co-design', which in practice means a firm developing its products in collaboration with its customers. Despite their lexical indigence and creative bankruptcy, the confection of such neologisms underlines, incidentally, the aspiration of business ideologues to set up a world of reference valid for all. The eulogy of diversity that they endlessly wheel out in various formats only possesses meaning in relation to that world; its resemblance to the ethnological discourse on cultural plurality is entirely superficial. In the final analysis it bears only on the production of consumer goods and any ability the consumers may have to modify them in marginal ways.

A second aspect of innovation is juridical. Patents on inventions, which in France date from the Revolution, concern 'new inventions embodying inventive activity and capable of use in industrial applications'; they do not cover scientific discoveries or theories. But the relation between innovation and law became complicated with the progress of research in biology, and the French law of 2004 on bioethics is liable to further change. The debate on the status of human embryos pits those who refuse to see it as a simple matter against those who, in the name of fundamental science or for economic reasons, fear that research teams may be forced to go abroad to pursue their work. Jacomy notes that the Supreme Court, in a 1981 decision, legalized the patenting of genetically modified bacteria. We may also think of the possible role of nanotechnologies in performance-enhancing modifications to the human body. It is plain that scientific investigation will raise further questions, not just in the ethical domain but in the domain of ecology and risk in general. The precautionary principle, so often invoked, can become a lifeline or a restraint depending on how it is used, and the question of the frontier between basic research and 'innovation', as in the launch of a new invention on the market, is crucial here.

A third aspect of innovation is economic. It occupies a growing place in what is now called the economics of knowledge. Corinne Autant-Bernard (*Innovation*, p. 12) writes that after Schumpeter, interest in innovation only reappeared in the 1960s in the US, stimulated by Kenneth Arrow and Richard Nelson, and she adds: 'The economics of innovation today constitutes a specific branch of economics, studying the process of innovation (i.e., creation of new products and services and new production methods), as well as the repercussions of innovation on economic activity (growth, employment, investment, exports etc.).' The author examines various technical facets of research in this field, including measuring innovation or innovativeness – a difficult thing to do – and the complex relations between size of company, industrial concentration, competing markets and 'propensity to innovate'. But what will concern us more specifically here is what I will call the totalizing conception of innovation and of research focused on it. Four main types of innovation can be distinguished, bearing respectively on products, production methods, modes of organization and marketing techniques. Examples of collaboration by state employees with private organizations, or by the state in training engineers, are arising in unprecedented profusion across the new landscape.

The rise of technology has always been associated with a vision of the world, and its history has seen great founding moments like the European Renaissance and, in the eighteenth century, the enterprise of the Encyclopaedists. But the humanist outlook and democratizing ambitions (which at those times did not just characterize but were integral to them) are today closely correlated with the corporate world. Hence, the call for participation of the human sciences in training engineers hired by industry: 'Training in innovation is effectively training in technical realization, but it also means thinking about the society in which the realization takes place. Developing an innovation doesn't only mean finding the "best" technological solution, it also has to be in phase with the expectations of the different parties (users, communities, manufacturers and so on).' This seems to come down to a 'disruption of the traditional cartography of knowledge' (Marianne Chouteau, Joëlle Forest, Céline Nguyen, *Innovation*, p. 43).

'Disruption' may seem a somewhat overblown term given that in the 1960s, following the wave of independences, all economic development operations in the former colonies relied on interdisciplinary collaborations of that very type. The innumerable studies emerging from the focus on the 'human factor' seemed to me to show the same slant as the new theories of innovation: under the pretext of adapting to society and studying the human milieu, they in fact displayed a clear wish to transform that milieu from top to bottom – it was more the promotion of an ideology than an analysis of reality. In other words, they were part of the reality they sought to study; the sign of the transformation whose conditions they were supposed to be investigating. Nevertheless some of these studies were first-rate, subtle documents that historians of the period will one day find useful.

We may wonder, similarly, if the accompaniment of the phenomenon of technological innovation by the human sciences is not an internal component rather than an external analysis. Society's dominant forces have understood the social dimension of their conquest of the planet, and understood at the same time the need to produce their own instruments to measure and assess their project. Not out of some sort of Machiavellian scheme to defraud those who would be both agents and objects of the plan, but because, specifically, the project is global, total, and cannot be conceived in a partial way. It may encounter setbacks or defeats (start-up financing hasn't always achieved as much as was hoped), but it is indelibly written into a global and intellectually totalitarian vision of the world.

What this means is that the public's 'expectations', which are supposedly fulfilled and which the system purports to measure, are really induced by the system in which the public participates as user and consumer. In those roles it may show astuteness and ingenuity; but that only underlines its triumphant integration by the system. A system that is not restricted to the narrow technical field, but that expresses a social, economic and political worldview.

Hence the two glaring paradoxes that surface in the literature on innovation. The first is the wide disparity of the examples cited in its favour: at one end of the scale, biodegradable supermarket bags, an improved kayak or ice-axe, and at the other IT, the web and 3D scannable medical imaging. The latter end highlights once again the effect of language that is in play here; while a whole literature is devoted to the scale of the phenomenon of innovation (Eric von Himmel asserts that two or three times as many innovations are due to users than to industry), Autant-Bernard notes their very unequal geographical distribution: 'So the bulk of innovation only takes place in a limited number of countries, and within those countries in a limited number of regions, mainly in the urban zones of those regions. Silicon Valley is a particularly striking example, and is often taken as a model for developing European technopoli' (*Innovation*, p. 15). It seems reasonable to wonder whether the word has the same meaning and the same range in all its uses. Sometimes it designates an ingenious procedure of improvement to existing techniques, of which there are countless examples from human history and its gamut of cultures; sometimes an unprecedented contemporary phenomenon, the marketing of original ideas derived from fundamental research.

So it seems very much as if the term 'innovation', used on its own, embodies above all the ideology of the neoliberal economy, a symbol of initiative, dynamism and perpetual renewal, applicable to techniques, to those who invent and deploy them, to all those who make use of them and to society in general.

Observation of new words and expressions is always a good indicator of this sort of trend. Not so long ago, 'enterprise culture' was in fashion. It could be understood in two ways. On the one hand, each enterprise was a society in itself with its own rules, way of life, history and solidarities: its own culture. On the other hand, it was a model of economic and social rationality that might profitably be followed by states. But lately the expression has been heard less often. Two aspects of the economic crisis seem to lie behind this new discretion. People had tended to forget that an enterprise has owners and/or shareholders, but were soon reminded, when it became necessary to choose between the bosses' and the workers' interests, that financial logic won out every time. Businesses generally chose to cut jobs rather than reduce executive fees and dividends; that is the price we must pay to maintain competitiveness, the bosses said in their own defence. But after that it became more difficult for them to celebrate the virtues of enterprise culture as an integral, interdependent milieu. On another level, certain political leaders claimed to be managing their countries like businesses, with lamentable results that did nothing to endorse their choice. 'Enterprise culture' is rather more exposed today as what it was in the first place: a word, an alibi, a weapon.

Today's buzzword is 'social media', used in the plural to express the multiplicity, diversity and plasticity of the reality to which it is applied. It refers in the first instance to the new communication techniques that emerged from the invention of the Web by CERN (European Organization for Nuclear Research). The innovative users mentioned in the literature on innovation are often internet users who communicate among themselves via networks of 'social media'. Such networking services have been much mentioned recently in connection with the 'Arab revolutions'; they were presented originally as the enterprise of technologically switched-on young people eager to free themselves from dictatorial regimes. Certainly the internet is an unprecedented means of communication, and may well have played a mobilizing role in some cases. But the crowds assembled in the squares of Tunis and Cairo did not look much like a cross-section of internet clients. The systematic harping by the traditional media on the term 'social media' has corresponded, up to a point, more with a wish than an observation: the wish for a revolution led by the young-est, one open to the most innovative aspects of liberal democracy, proof through historical experience of the theory of the end of history: the spontaneous and miracu-lous upsurge of the model that military force tried vainly for years to impose on Iraq and Afghanistan.

History is often ironic. 'Social media' were mentioned a number of times in connection with the riots seen a few years ago in areas of North London. We were told that the rioting gangs communicated via mobile phones and the internet to evade the police and anticipate their moves. But by trying to give a social dimension to simple tools of communication, we risk promoting a banal urban riot into a revolutionary movement . . . Return to sender, as it were. And perhaps a salutary return, given that lack of a viable future seemed to be the predominant feeling among the rioters in London and other British towns.

Innovation is not always immediately recognizable and there is something odd, during the current economic crisis, in the widespread expressions of astonishment (from President Obama downward) at the downgrading of the US economy's credit rating by a 'rating agency'. It has to be said that until very recently, we ordinary consumers were unaware that such institutions existed and did not know what they were called. Not until a few months ago were we told of their existence by the media, along with the details of their rating system and of their considerable influence. Will France lose its AAA rating? The question would have meant nothing to the public just two or three years ago; now, suddenly, people are worried or angered by the idea of a possible slashed rating. Carol Sirou, a French representative of Standard & Poor's, was very revealing on the growing role of these agencies in an interview with *Libération* (8 August 2011): 'Everyone seems to be discovering our existence. But we've been rating businesses and states for decades. What has changed is that investment funds, banks and insurance companies have added our ratings to their internal rules. In other words a particular fund, for example, will require itself to place X per cent of its investments in AAA-rated equities, Y per cent in AA, and so on, and be obliged to sell them if their ratings fall. That gave us, at a stroke, a systemic role we never had before. One that has the effect of an accelerator. So the market is forcing us to play a role which isn't really ours.' What is new in this business, then, is a change not in the way rating agencies work, but in the strategy of institutions which exercise decisive influence on the market. The change is interesting in two ways: it is itself an innovation, in the officially accepted meaning of the word, and it reveals the true nature of planetary power at present, which is essentially financial.

By the same token, it invites us to exercise intellectual vigilance. Systematic use of words whose meanings one has not mastered, the mechanical repetition of ready-made formulae, are behaviours that characterize magic. And the ability of the media to impose them and spread them across the planet in a few days is terrifying. Because these words and formulae have a meaning; they speak the truth about the world; but that truth escapes us nevertheless, and those who enjoy its benefits have the impunity of limited liability companies. Globalization is more perverse than colonization in that its actors are less easily identifiable even though it is imposed on everyone. We all have the feeling that we are colonized but we do not know who by, if not by apparently abstract entities with terribly concrete effects: Market, Stock Exchange, Crisis, Growth, Employment, Investors and Economic Agents. They have replaced the Destiny and Fate which under various names have always had a place in human mythologies. It is hard here to resist the temptation to quote Marx's image of an 'enchanted, perverted, topsy-turvy world, in which Monsieur le Capital and Madame la Terre do their ghost-walking as social characters and at the same time directly as mere things.' (*Capital*, Book III, Chapter 48).

Chapter 7
Bet on the Future: Meaning, Faith, Science

It often happens that after giving a talk in which I have mentioned the more discouraging aspects of the present world (and we all know that these are not lacking), someone will summon the courage to ask me: 'So what should be done?' or even, with a hint of impatience or irritation, 'So what's your suggestion?' I hear the question, but I know full well that it is not addressed to me, that it is not even a real question, and that if I made a considered reply the questioner would be dumbfounded or even incredulous.

What is to be done? The interrogative title of Lenin's booklet still continues to provoke us, and it is interesting to hear the question reiterated in our own time, in which everything is in doubt. Especially the great visions of the future sketched out in the nineteenth century, which claimed countless millions of victims when the time came to 'put them into practice'. Also in doubt are the peripheral implications of the neoliberal 'grand narrative' and its ideal (representative democracy and market economy), given its setbacks whether technical (growing inequalities), political (non-democratic regimes have a hard life) or ideological (God brought into every mix by totalitarianisms of every stripe). Answering the question 'what is to be done?' which concerns the immediate future, means exposure, under present conditions, to the risk of pious wishes and more or less abstract reflection. Apart from that, answering the question exposes me personally to the risk of repeating myself; for I have already tried sometimes to outline an answer and cannot reasonably or morally change it, persuaded though I am of its imprecisions, of its programmatic deficiencies and, things being what they are today, of its unrealistic character. I will attempt however, by way of a necessarily provisional conclusion, to specify an answer (that is the whole gamble of this book), very modestly, but with the hope, if nothing more, of closing in effectively on the meaning of the question and what is at stake.

First of all, I would recall that the question of knowledge is essential to the definition of our future, meaning the future of the planet and of humanity.

It is essential for various sets of reasons. We could start by thinking that knowledge of the effects that the development of human societies are having on the planet they inhabit is crucial for their future. But what I would like to examine here is another aspect of things, even though of course it is linked to that one. In this area, everything is connected.

Let us start from two observations. The first is that science is developing at increasing speed and our imagination is powerless to keep up. We are unable today to give an accurate prediction of the state of science fifty or even thirty years hence. By the state of science, I mean both our level of knowledge and its practical side effects on human life. We are faced with an immense zone of uncertainty, about which specialists can produce any number of hypotheses and projections without being able to state anything for sure, apart from the certainty that they will one day be surprised by what turns up.

The accelerating advance of science since the beginning of the twentieth century leaves us today facing revolutionary prospects. New worlds are being opened up: on one hand the universe and its myriad galaxies (and the vertiginous change of scale that goes with them, which will eventually alter the idea we have of the planet and of humanity); on the other, the frontier between matter and life, the inner secrets of living beings, the nature of consciousness (new ideas which will lead to a redefinition of the idea individuals have of themselves).

The second observation is that inequality is even greater in science than it is in economic matters.

In the economic domain, the system of globalization is marked by a growing gap between the richest and the poorest. This increasing gap can be seen even in the developed countries themselves. It is more marked still in emergent countries like China or India, where the corollary of their access to the world market is an internal accentuation of the gap between the very rich and the very poor. This global inequality is gradually replacing the traditional North/South opposition, although this remains pertinent: the fact is that social welfare policies remain a lot more efficient and systematic in the developed northern countries, while migratory flows move from South to North and South to South, but not from North to South.

In the scientific domain the situation is more drastic still. As in the economic field, new poles of development are appearing (China, India). But the internal gaps are colossal in the 'scientifically emergent' countries. They are widening, incidentally, in the developed countries too. The reason for this is that scientific research today requires an existing accumulation of financial and intellectual capital. Such concentration exists only in a few scattered places on the planet. George Steiner noted some years ago now that the research budget of Harvard University alone was greater than the sum of the research budgets of all the European universities. What seems to be taking shape on the horizon is a dual-level inequality, between different countries (it is unthinkable that Rwanda could ever acquire the scientific potential of the US) and within countries, developed and undeveloped alike. One can also note, in this connection, that the situation of internal imbalance prevents the most developed countries from mounting consistent plans for scientific and intellectual aid to the less developed (they still have too much to do at home), while on the other hand the most intellectually distinguished elements in poor countries, for example in Africa, have little choice but to emigrate permanently. The brain drain and the individualization of scientific careers are characteristic of globalization in the same way as mass migratory flows.

Given all of that, there seems to be good reason to worry about the future. A world oligarchy of power, money and knowledge has seized the controls of the planet, and a prospect very different from the one imagined by theorists of the 'end of history' is becoming more real by the day. In any case, for the moment, representative democracy does not appear to be the necessary corollary of the neoliberal market. Is real neoliberalism doomed to meet the same fate as 'real socialism'? Is the 'end of history' to be the last of the 'grand narratives'?

Let us return for a moment to the notion suggested by Lyotard. The myths of origin, the cosmologies whose presence is recorded in the history of all human groups, were conceived to give a meaning to the world. Lévi-Strauss expands this very well in his *Introduction à l'œuvre de Marcel Mauss*: from the first appearance of language, the universe has been required to signify. This signifying was achieved through an arbitrary distribution of meaning and symbolism on the world. Meaning, thus defined as the commanding principle of the social, of group life and social relations, is not knowledge, but it is the precondition for all knowledge possible within a universe and a society themselves conceived as closed entities.

Traditional knowledge, for example 'native medicine', fits into that concept of meaning. This is not to say that some of its practices and classifications are not based on empirical observation. On the contrary, ethnologists have always been struck by the accuracy and exhaustiveness of the accounts given by all human groups of their natural surroundings; likewise their views on human psychology. But the ethnopsychiatrist George Devereux noted that the Mojave Indians, even though they attributed psychological meaning to dreams and psychoses, had not arrived at a general theory of psychopathology because their basic orientation was towards a priori (therefore unscientific) forms of construction. Out of the cosmologies or grand narratives of the distant past, what we see is the development of practical modalities for management of everyday life, partial technical knowledge derived from observation of nature (effects of certain plants, regularity of the seasons, recurrence of celestial configurations) and 'popular wisdom' which, in the Western tradition, is stored in the form of proverbs. One might call it an art of living.

These forms of wisdom do not exclude a hierarchical ordering of society – far from it – and they are conservative. They are passed on as a tradition. As for the real knowledge involved, that too is passed on and may also be diffused through society, but it does not progress or develop. It is rooted in cosmologies fixed once and for all.

Societies that subscribe to that definition of meaning are polytheistic.

Monotheism adds faith to meaning. Traditional meaning survives in monotheistic societies, as paganism in Christian or Muslim societies, and in various forms. Monotheism brings two new and complementary elements: individual faith, which has little place in polytheistic logic; an idea of the individual and collective future which is virtually unknown in polytheism; and lastly, in consequence, proselytism, which implies both a universalist conception of nature and a conquering conception of history.

When we say that eighteenth-century modernity, scientific modernity, has done away with the grand narratives of the past to make room for future ones, we are forgetting too readily the eschatological dimension of monotheistic religions. It is true that this is not strictly speaking a social dimension: it addresses both the fate of the individual after death, and the end of the world. Nevertheless, Muslim proselytism contains a very specific vision of the organization of society, which it aims in principle to extend to the entire world. Islamic fundamentalism is therefore a hybrid form: unlike the models of the nineteenth-century utopias, the model it seeks to apply is one that already exists.

Between traditional wisdoms and the proselytizing and reactionary pretensions of fundamentalist religion, the declension of cosmologies from the past results in some very different historical and conceptual situations.

It is true, of course, that the progressive utopias of the nineteenth century had tried to reverse the movement by projecting their own myths (such as the classless society) into the future. It was over a period of time that they thought of changing the world. In that respect they differed from the monotheisms. But the vision they projected was of a finished whole that presupposed the existence of an already directed past, of something in the past that authorized a projection into the future. The detailed mental sketch that prefigured the totality to come did not have the status of a scientific hypothesis. Historic socialism is not scientific, because it has an idea of the end (in both senses of the word). When presented as a key to deciphering social relations it resembles the logics of meaning, but when it outlines the shape of the future it bears a clear resemblance to the logics of faith. In the final analysis it hovers midway between the two, for better or worse, with something like what has been called the optimism of the will.

When Lyotard attributed the appearance of the postmodern condition to the death of the grand narratives of modernity, he was referring us back to obvious aspects and realities of the present, notably the existence of networks of all sorts in terms of which one might be tempted to define postmodernity; to the world of instantaneousness and ubiquity analysed by Paul Virilio. But we cannot think about the present outside time without making it into an ideology, and the notion of postmodernity, purely descriptive of a moment or a dawning awareness, finally has meaning only in relation to what precedes it. It is a notion that halts time.

The practice of science involves meaning, faith and volition, but does not arise from them primarily. It does not start from meaning, it does not follow faith and it does not deny what resists it. We need meaning, insofar as we need to think through our relation to others (no identity is constructed without reference to otherness). But when all relations are prescribed, freedom and identity can no longer exist: the excess of meaning kills both. We need faith, to the extent that we need to believe in what we are doing. But when faith stands in for certainty and orders the acts instead of proceeding from them, when it does not learn from experience and short-circuits reflection, it is denying all otherness in the name of an arbitrarily postulated identity. We need volition, if only to live and keep thinking; but voluntarism can blind us to reality.

Excesses of meaning, faith and volition all stem from a principled reference, arbitrarily postulated, to the whole; they reject the unknown, in other words reality. The notion of mystery, in Christianity, proceeds from a short-circuit of thought, an intellectual fait accompli placing the unknown in the domain of the known through recourse to such notions as prophecy, annunciation or revelation.

Compared with such demonstrations of vainglory, science is a model of modesty. The history of science is that of the gradual pushing back, with corrections, failures and rectifications, of the frontiers of the unknown. Time and the unknown underlie the existence of science and its method. Science works from established knowledge, but never considers it definitive given that advances in the way it interprets reality may cause it to reconsider at any time.

In other words, the only sector of human activity in which the notion of progress, in the sense of an accumulation of knowledge, is borne out by the reality is also the one in which notions of certainty, truth and totality are incessantly questioned and re-examined. For this reason alone, the scientific approach may be considered the model of what any initiative in the political or social field ought to be. Not to rule in the name of science (there is no absolute original knowledge), but with science in view. It is the inverse and opposite of all fundamentalisms, whether jihadi or creationist. Science produces forms of plot development which do not flow mechanically from what precedes them. Epistemological breaks may mark the consequences of the limits of earlier models, but in all cases an imagination of the future, inductive rather than deductive, plays an essential part. Sartre (*Situations I, La Liberté cartésienne*) admired the boldness with which Descartes approached the unknown, and noted of the *Discourse on Method* that most of the rules on method were maxims 'of action and invention', adding: 'Was not Descartes, at a time when Bacon was teaching the English to look to experience, the first to call upon the physicist to give precedence to hypothesis?'

The construction of hypotheses is today the most exciting task physicists have, and exploration of the inner structures of matter seems complementary, or identical, to exploration of the infinite universe. Science is today the only field of human activity generating plotlines whose potential importance and interest can be appreciated by everyone, without of course understanding all the content or even all the implications. Much energy has been devoted in recent times to the quest for the Higgs boson, the elementary particle whose existence supposedly confirms that of the Higgs field, thus helping to fill one of the last remaining gaps in the Standard Model. That hypothesis is based on close observation of otherwise inexplicable facts, as far back as Le Verrier's discovery of the planet Neptune in 1846. The main objective of the huge CERN particle accelerator was to prove the existence of the boson, which had never been observed for certain. This time the task would not be just to observe, but to construct (at great cost) the experimental apparatus needed to test the hypothesis. Some even hoped that the Large Hadron Collider might produce evidence of 'dark matter', particles of a matter that does not emit, reflect or absorb light. The ignoramus can derive three lessons from all this. First, that the ambition and the modesty of science are both cut from the same cloth. Nothing could be more modest than a physicist explaining that failure to prove the existence of the Higgs boson would be disappointing, certainly, but the immediate task would be to construct more hypotheses. At the same time, what could be more vertiginous than the ambition of a programme aiming to connect the physics of the infinitely small with that of the infinitely vast, one which, if it is completed, could give birth to a new physics? Lastly, without idealizing the individuals concerned, it should be noted that the scientific community offers the spectacle of a transnational coalition of endeavour, apparent in the diverse origins of the researchers working at CERN and in its fruitful collaboration with its US equivalent, Fermilab. The twenty European member-states are actively helped by such countries as Australia, Brazil and China, and by Japan, Russia and the US which have observer status.

In view of the goals pursued by scientific communities

and the types of cooperation they have managed to establish to that effect, it seems inexplicable that we are not more tempted to see their example as a model and a hope for humanity as a whole.

It is true that the existence of aggressive forms of religiosity (Islamism, evangelism) can make us fear a twenty-first century torn apart by conflicting and equally backward conceptions of the world, which would contradict the theme of the end of myths of origin and of future myths. It is true that, without overestimating the capacity of religious fundamentalisms to impose their worldviews, we should nevertheless not underestimate their literally reactionary character. Modernity remains to be conquered, and we are in the midst of a crisis whose ideological dimension it would be wrong to ignore. On the other hand, there is a positive side to the indisputable slackening or even disappearance of large-scale political projections; for in the end, that absence of constructed representations of the future could give us a real chance to devise changes on the basis of concrete historical experience.

Perhaps we are in the process of learning to change the world before imagining it, converting to a sort of political and practical existentialism. The technological innovations that revolutionized sexual relations and modes of communication (contraceptive pill, internet) were not born of a utopia, but of science and its technological fallout, and these things have transformed our relation to the world. We now need to turn towards the future without projecting our illusions into it, to forge hypotheses and test their validity, and learn to push back gradually and prudently the frontiers of the unknown: that is what science teaches us, what every educational programme should promote and what ought to inspire any and every reflection of a political nature.

Democratic necessity and individual assertion will perhaps take unprecedented paths tomorrow that we can still hardly glimpse today.

Chapter 8
An Educational Utopia

It is on that foundation that what I have sometimes called an educational utopia should be constructed. Little by little, step by step, but without losing sight of the end purpose it would be trying to serve.

This is a domain where it is important to speak seriously. Affirmations and figures (for example a school attendance level) are not enough; they can even serve as cover for the most culpable failings. It is certainly important for children to get schooling, but it is also important not to teach them just any old rubbish. Keeping them in class without teaching them anything, or imprisoning and indoctrinating them, should not be confused with the ideal of generalized education.

One might imagine that in a society whose goal is knowledge with prosperity as a consequence, social injustices would be considered intellectually piffling, economically wasteful and scientifically damaging. A model could be conceived, in the scientists' sense, to try to verify or refine this hypothesis. Besides, it has already been established, albeit on a very small scale, that culturally and economically deprived groups in which a practical effort has been made for women's education and training have seen their situations improve noticeably. But, to tell the truth, this kind of 'verification' is pretty useless. Not only because, as so often, the experimental setup merely demonstrates the obvious, but much more because broad development of education is a general categorical imperative which has no need to be propped up by any blather about economic profitability: it is an end in itself, in the name of the unity of the human species – an axiomatic principle; but there are also good reasons to think that its first consequences would include economic prosperity.

The educational utopia is the only remaining hope of redirecting human history towards its ends. The term 'utopia' may seem worrying. In fact, in this usage, the word has meaning only in relation to current policies which are all tending the wrong way, whatever is claimed for them: they are resigned to educational failure, link school and university too closely with the matter of employment, do not try hard enough to create the conditions for a general culture independent of family or social background, and overall ignore the question of ends or restrict it to the economic field, for example by asserting that a return to growth is an absolute precondition for any new social initiative. But this 'utopia' has its place: the entire earth, the whole planet; with a touch of optimism, I will call it a programme. The programme can – indeed, it must – adapt to the passing political time, to the long term which would become a form of hope, were there the slightest sign of progress towards its application . . . Today there is none, but something could start to take shape tomorrow.

A programme of that sort obviously could not be the

result of any wish to govern *in the name* of an absolute knowledge. Knowledge, in contrast to ideology, is neither a totality nor a starting point. Such a programme would, on the contrary, govern *with a view* to learning, adopting knowledge as an individual and collective purpose, destined to remain prospective and asymptotic. It is most regrettable that the term 'scientism' should be so often and so loosely employed by polemicists, aware or unaware of the resonances this word possesses. No scientist can be called scientistic if scientism signifies the assertion of a total knowledge from which the correct behaviour of men in society can be deduced. If, on the other hand, the word expresses the conviction – shared by all scientists – that the human mind has the capacity to make indefinite progress in learning, including knowledge of the cerebral mechanisms making this progress possible, then to use it in a polemical way is to resort to bad faith and obscurantism pure and simple.

Today we are being told, excitedly, that a lot of young people are in fact uneducated. People fret about what forms of apprenticeship should accompany schooling to ensure a painless transition towards the world of labour; they worry that educational backlogs are accumulating, and some children enter secondary school who have not mastered the three Rs; that after the first year of university, too many students drop out; that the universities do not cooperate with business well enough to find ready outlets for their students.

I understand of course that those responsible, at all levels, have to face difficult concrete situations, and I can't claim to have any ready-made solutions for now. The fact remains that at a time when demands for profitability are cited to justify job cuts, resulting in a decline in purchasing power which causes a slowdown in growth (one of the vicious circles of capitalism in its present phase), education policies are becoming less and less focused on the acquisition of learning for its own sake. Selection takes place younger and younger, and children from 'economically deprived' backgrounds, to use the current euphemism, have little or no chance of acceding to certain types of education. Sociologists have pointed out that in a country like France, the education system nowadays tends to reproduce social inequalities, instead of reducing them. Admittedly we are in an age of higher education for the many, but the drop-out level in the first two years is considerable. And opening the universities to the many is officially considered to change their vocation: they are being asked to prioritize the needs of the labour market.

I return then to the use of the word utopia, since it should serve to recall some principles, outline an ideal, suggest a few promising paths and avoid some blockages. The theme of educational utopia reprises the old arguments which have punctuated European history since the Renaissance. For Montaigne what mattered was pedagogy in general, but for Rousseau it was the ideal education of a singular, exemplary subject. In his reflection on intellectuals (*Situations VIII*), Sartre in 1966 changed perspective by considering the category of 'technicians of practical learning' from which they are recruited, and the training these technicians have themselves received, but his comment was not intended to be pedagogical. 1966 was a time of relative economic prosperity, and Sartre's radical critical thought was whetted on such contemporary phenomena as class struggle, colonialism, imperialism, racism and sexism. Half a century later, the same issues remain present, in different terms; but it is still possible that this slippage over time may help people to acquire, through distance, a clearer awareness of what is really at stake in education policy.

Sartre attempts to define the characteristics shown – at the time when he was writing the text, originally a lecture given in Japan between September and October 1966 – by the 'social category' of those he calls the 'technicians of practical knowledge'.

In his view, the ruling class bears prime responsibility. It decides on the jobs that will be occupied by those technicians (doctors, teachers and so on), their numbers, their level of specialization and their distribution. For a whole category of adolescents, this signifies '[a structuring of the field of possibilities, what subjects to study and, beyond that, a destiny]'. When making its choices, the ruling class takes into account the state of industrial growth, the conjuncture, and some of the new requirements that have appeared – advertising, 'human engineering' and so on. In short, Sartre was formulating, before the word existed or its use given the seal of approval, a summary of the theory of innovation in a social context, accompanied by a far-sighted observation which forty-five years on we can confirm: '[Today, the thing is clear: industry wants to lay hold of the university to compel it to abandon outmoded old humanism and replace it with specialized disciplines, intended to provide enterprises with test engineers, middle managers and the like.]'

Next, Sartre examines the technical and ideological training these specialists in practical knowledge have received from the education system (secondary and tertiary) imposed on them 'from on high'. In the first place, he says, it assigns and teaches them two roles: it makes them 'research specialists', certainly, but also '[servants of the hegemony]' or, to use Gramsci's expression, '[functionaries of the superstructures]'.

Lastly, Sartre notes that class relations rule the selection of these technicians automatically. There are hardly any promoted workers among them; the system only allows the working class to make the transition under exceptional circumstances. They are recruited mainly from among the children of petty-bourgeois families inculcated since childhood (in primary and secondary school) with the particularistic ideology of the ruling class. The fate of the technician of practical knowledge was determined from the start by the ruling class, which decided notably what share of surplus to devote to his salary in view of the conjuncture and the growth situation: ['In that sense, his social being and his destiny come from outside: he is the man of means, the average man, the middle-class man; the general purposes to which his activity is bent are not *his* purposes.']

Sartre's analyses, which bear the stamp of their time and whose language is distinctly dated, are still fascinating for their definition of the intellectual as one who 'interferes in what doesn't concern him': a reproach often addressed to him from outside, but one he can brush off in all conscience, being convinced that on the contrary, all of that *does* 'concern him'. The Sartrean intellectual is a technician of the universal '[who realizes that, in his specific field, universality does not exist ready-made, that it is perpetually under construction]'. Unlike the eighteenth-century philosophers, who embodied the requirements of the bourgeoisie to which they belonged and were in that respect 'organic intellectuals' in Gramsci's sense, the Sartrean is a man of insight, aware of the co-presence within him of both singular and universal, who cannot hope to attain universality except by embracing his singularity. The intellectual knows which social class he comes from, and has to conduct a critical analysis to liberate himself from it; like Flaubert, he has to make an effort to escape, not from the past which makes his 'singularity', but from determination by that past: '[Real intellectual research, which aims to expose the myths that obscure it, implies a passage by the investigation through the investigator's singularity]'. This principle (which might have been formulated by an anthropologist who, when he gets down to thinking about his object of investigation, has to start by bringing himself into the thought process), is clearly aimed at neutralizing prejudices stemming from social class and occupation – all the class and professional alienations that interfere with freedom of analysis, observation and decision. Sartre illustrates this philosophy of freedom with two overlapping quotations, one from Ponge ('Man is the future of man') and the other from Malraux ('A life is worth nothing, but nothing is worth a life'). The latter quote makes ambivalence the essence of the literary work, and the literary work itself an expression of the ever-fertile contradiction between the particular and the universal.

Sartre is a remarkable analyst and brilliant dialectician, but most of all he was carried along by a voluntaristic momentum in the aftermath of the Second World War. In the immediate post-war period, people thought they could change society and establish the foundations of a new solidarity: they believed in the future. Of course there were rifts, with a powerful Communist Party arousing opposition on many sides, but collaborations had been outlined too, and above all it was unthinkable, after such a punishing, *mutilating* ordeal, not to look towards a different horizon. Literature and cinema both bear witness to that state of mind, which obliged people to leave behind the horrors of the war and Nazism, on the historical level, and on the metaphysical plane to transcend, if necessary through an ethic of heroism, the sense of absurdity engendered by man's confrontation with the silence of the world. Camus springs naturally to mind, and existentialism: to affirm that existence comes before essence is to define man as his own creator.

The world's horrors have lost none of their intensity; but today we are not emerging from an ordeal as fundamental, identifiable and symbolic as that suffered during the Second World War. Until proofs to the contrary, economic crises lead to anxiety, depression and uncontrolled violence, but not to intellectual great leaps forward. That is why the educational utopia is utopian: it is not sufficiently adjusted to the period to impose itself as an obvious development.

However, a few apparently contradictory signs seem to suggest it would be a good idea. The youth revolts in various urban areas on different continents cannot be said to constitute a direct demand for reform of the education system, but nor are they mere explosions of violence, or reactions to poverty. Insofar as they express the injustice of a situation of social marginalization, they are really a quest for truth: what ought society to be, since it evidently fails to define itself in terms of a community of destinies? The theme of exclusion (social, economic, intellectual) carries its opposite within it: what ought social *inclusion* to be like? Every social protest has its reverse side, which is the fundamental question: what is the social bond? Every protest is a form of research.

Another sign, more directly decipherable, is the appetite for knowledge evinced by the public whenever the opportunity arises. Italy is an especially remarkable example, given the large number of cultural festivals and gatherings organized there and enthusiastically attended. Even in France, where such initiatives are fewer, the experimental Université de tous les savoirs was immensely successful, and various 'Popular Universities', of which the best-known is in Caen, have a significant following. Overall, in Europe at least, the impression prevails of an immense reservoir of unused intellectual capacity. This engenders widespread feelings of frustration and injustice, a hole which cannot be filled either by the uninterrupted torrent of random information on television ('There may be water on Mars', 'Paris Saint-Germain has purchased five new players') or by invitations to Net users to comment in their own way on the latest news of the day.

Utopia: the first merit of this word is that it compels us to look to the future. Its second merit is that it invites us, at least in the name of provisional morality, to pay no attention to the myriad arguments that may be marshalled against it, short of simply regarding them, in Sartre's straightforward but effective language, as utterances of the 'ruling class': what we might call the prevailing system.

Practical, pragmatic utopia, progressive but gradual: these adjectives matter because they govern the possibility of a passage to effective action. A revolution on that scale can only be accomplished at the end of a controlled, measured and (if necessary) amended and reformed *evolution*. A few principles might soon begin to take shape. To address educational failure, the size of certain 'difficult' primary school classes ought to be reduced to four or five pupils. The same measure could be applied for a few years – as long as it takes for the primary school reform to start working – at secondary level. These measures would obviously involve recruiting extra teachers.

The syllabus would be planned along broad-based, fundamental lines. Selection into scientific, literary or mixed streams would be left as late as possible, until the fourth or fifth forms. Courses in two European languages would be compulsory in all streams.

A broad programme of scholarships for school accommodation and residential arrangements for secondary pupils would open up secondary education by enabling willing pupils from poor families to live autonomously and attend their school of choice. For younger children, it would be necessary to devise boarding arrangements to help needy families meet the financial and cultural burden. This last measure would be very costly, and imply further heavy recruitment.

Once this programme really took root, there would be no specific need for basic reform of the university system (even though things might vary from country to country, and it would be essential, in all circumstances, to supervise closely the award of grants to students, on economic criteria, and recruitment policies, on academic criteria). One point is worth emphasizing, however. Universities must preserve the vocation which their name implies. Their autonomy should not be allowed to transform them into mere appendages of big business. What universities must continue to provide is a fundamental training driven solely by the quest for knowledge. Obviously, firms can make contact with universities to explain their staffing needs, but it should be up to the enterprises themselves to ensure any necessary complementary training. Broadly speaking, the distinction between fundamental and applied research is useful to both. In some sectors the distinction is fading or disappearing, fundamental physics for example being unable to advance without the very costly instruments now being perfected. But it is the end purpose of pure knowledge that people must keep in mind when they are running a university.

I have raised these few (obviously arguable) points for a possible programme, rapidly and superficially, not to start a debate which would obviously be premature in the current conditions, but rather to underline a simple, commonsensical truth: in the name of 'utopia', it is quite possible to propose partial and concrete reforms that would be wholly achievable. The ethnologist as such analyses existing situations; his vocation is not that of the prophet, even if he has sometimes had to study characters who claimed that title and function. But the world in which we live teems with messages claiming to provide the key to the present by assessing the recent past (yesterday is already history) and the near future (tomorrow is already today). Are these messages expressions of truth or are they confecting, a little at a time, the mythology and ideology of the global world of which we are part?

That question is more familiar to the ethnologist. He knows that behind constructed visions of the future there usually lies nothing more than the failings and fears of the present. We are not obliged to admit those failings and fears, let alone share them. We have the right not to buy the arrogant discourse of politicians more anxious to punish the thefts of a few rioters than to reform the education system and social system. We have the right – and some would say the duty – to withhold our trust from people who ask us to make sacrifices in a situation of inequality which they do their very best to protect, reproduce and enlarge. In sum, we have the right to remain free to observe, to make judgments and to distrust some of the words whose use is forced on us.

Insurance and credit are two ostensibly antinomic economic elements, two contrary modes of relation to the future. I insure myself against all the risks of life; if I am insured, nothing serious can befall me. I can even protect my nearest and dearest: 'if something happens to me', as the saying goes, my family will get some money. I can even specify the details of my funeral. Thus the entire course of life appears marked out, ordered, controlled like a heavily policed motorway during a holiday rush. Insurance is a defence against the accidents of life, the opposite of adventure.

Credit, by contrast, is open to the future. To live on credit is to show confidence in life, to take risks, listen to one's desires, satisfy them and pay later. It is to complete one's projects, in other words to bring the distant future attached to the notion of savings (I save in order to be able to live later) into the immediate present. In this sense credit is the opposite of investment, which brings an eventual return. It is deferred expenditure, the obverse or other face, since there are lenders who sell credit to borrowers.

But in reality, in financial terms, things are not that simple. Insurance is a financial product like any other, and insurance company shares are quoted on the stock exchange. Apart from that, credit is generally insured, while some equity investments are quite risky.

Even in psychological terms, things are not that simple. Insurance does not eliminate the accidents of life, it just provides financial means to help deal with them. It involves imagining in advance a life loaded with ever more catastrophic events, a life perpetually threatened by car crashes, burglaries and illnesses. The theoretical life of the insured is an adventurer's life. But nothing insures us against boredom. Credit, on the other hand, is a sort of dangerously concrete prefiguration of the future. By satisfying a desire immediately, credit eliminates it from view, consumes and corrodes it. It kills the imagination twice, by laying the mediocrity of our wishes for the future before our eyes. A car or a house, once they are no longer an aspiration or project, enter the domain of harsh everyday reality. Instead of dreaming, you have to run them, manage them . . . and repay the loan.

In fact, both credit and insurance offer us asepticized versions of the plot outline and the inauguration. They effectively marshal our desires and fears, channel and direct them. They are purveyors of illusions – illusions of protection or illusions of the future, it's all one. The only real adventurers in the consumer society are those who pull its strings, sometimes to breaking point, thus saddling their victims with a new narrative in which normally discreet and retiring characters appear in the foreground: markets (always feverish), traders (always dodgy), sovereign wealth funds (always badly managed). The various acts of this new narrative have frightening names: Debt, Crisis, Recession. Crisis scenarios are always much the same: they produce and direct, with great fanfare, alarm about the immediate future; but the moment the markets calm down, or become less feverish (nothing beats medical terminology when it comes to describing financial movements), everything can carry on as before. The system's ultimate ruse is to change a few words while repeating the same old story, to persuade those it has impoverished that through their sacrifices they will become the artisans of a fresh beginning. Credit and Insurance, the two faces of the economic Janus, will then look inviting once again, while awaiting the next crisis and its new fears.

Concerning education and the future, it is surely time to drop the economic metaphor ('education is an investment in the future', etc.). We should stop referring to the general interest, which often cloaks sectional interest, and start rather, not strictly speaking from the individual interest, but from the generic interest. It is by admitting the demands of the individual who is, in Sartre's language, both singular and universal; by admitting the share of generic humanity he carries within him (to which all education effort is addressed), that we may have a chance of recasting society.

Chapter 9
By Way of Provisional Conclusion: The Ethnologist and the Adventure of Knowledge

At the end of this journey, after considering the shadows that loom over our collective future, after sketching in a voluntaristic way some of the broad outlines of a possible programme, I must come back to the distinctions which introduced this text. The future of every individual is his or her death, and no resort to the future perfect (I will have been such and such a person, I will have done this or that) can alter that. To deal with that demise, as attractive and fascinating to man as it is repellent, we know that throughout history the most improbable myths were conjured up. But was their purpose to talk about death or to teach people to live? On the state of death they had nothing to say, and that is where their truth lies, perhaps: there is nothing to say about what does not exist. The great pagan intuition, expressed as much in birth rituals as in phenomena of possession, is that individuality is plural, made up of elements destined to dissolve and recompose, that everything is always beginning again; it is a scientific insight, in the sense that it eliminates at a stroke the hypotheses of individual immortality and of the existence of death.

The great Christian intuition – so long as the terms are inverted, and it is accepted that God was conceived in man's image – is that each individual existence is singular, distinct and unique; that too is a scientific insight. No doubt, too, the Judeo-Christian intuition could be credited with linking the advent of mankind with that of the desire for knowledge; but, here again, the terms would have to be inverted, the idea of evolution substituted for that of creation, and original sin made into humanity's end purpose and ultimate promise.

When we postulate that man's (any man's) essential vocation is knowledge, knowledge of what is, and of what man is, we are not saddling him with an unattainable ideal, ignoring the affective and material conditions needed for his well-being (and sometimes, happiness); we are acknowledging the share of generic humanity carried by everyone, and the ethical and critical requirement that flows from it. Including oneself in the knowledge of what is (the ethnologist's multiple journeys make the task easier) means making progress, embarking on a route and understanding that the movement itself is both the means to knowledge and its object. What am I, if not this fragile and tenacious will to understand? Shared awareness of this private tension defines the highest level of sociability, the most intense relation to others, the encounter.

So it will surprise no one if I conclude this reflection on the future by recalling my own journeys. Not that they were especially remarkable, but, in view of my profession, they did give me, over time, the opportunity to perceive with increasing clarity the overlapping of individual destinies swept along by the changes now taking place. They were simultaneously (as they are for everyone, but the ethnologist has particularly reliable references) a personal adventure (an expectation of events, an exploration of the future) and a historical (and in that sense, collective) experience. You can be an ethnologist without travelling, and travel without doing ethnology. It so happens that I have practised both of these activities in close conjunction, sometimes by accident, but always by choice. I realize today that in so doing I have been, along with a few others, a sort of witness, half-aware and half-unaware to start with, to the world's changes as it moved from colonization to globalization.

In my last book, *La Vie en double*, I identified three sorts of ethnology: residential ethnology, travelling ethnology and encounter ethnology. Allow me to expand for a moment on this distinction which plays a part in composing what, after Sartre, I might call my 'singularity'.

Residential ethnology is the version that corresponds to the traditional image of the ethnologist spending long months in the field, observing behaviour, taking note of the smallest details and interviewing informants, and eventually producing the most detailed portrait possible of a human group relatively identified by its location, language and culture. This was the task to which I had been harnessed in Côte d'Ivoire during the 1960s, among the Alladian people. Travelling anthropology starts from the fact that all identification is relative, and tries to bring a number of variables into play. I tried to work on that aspect after leaving the small Alladian group to study, all round the Ébrié lagoon which extends for dozens of kilometres to the west of Abidjan, other groups which were clearly different, but whose modes of organization could be compared to the ones I had studied first, enabling their anthropological meaning and what was at stake to be pinned down more easily. I could also employ the term travelling anthropology to cover my dealings with 'healer prophets' in Côte d'Ivoire, those colourful characters striving to understand and explain to their followers and patients the upheavals of a history knocked sideways by the colonial invasion which affected the social body as well as individual bodies. They were all of a kind, but each was unique. The existing literature made it possible to extend the trip into the Congo and South Africa, where phenomena and personages of the same nature had been studied. In Togo in the 1970s I examined some other variables, religious this time, as polytheist cults, officially banned in Côte d'Ivoire, were very actively and officially present there.

Encounter ethnology is more a matter of chance. Relative chance, though, for the itineraries followed by researchers and the demands that may be made on them are obviously linked to their previous work. It was thus that in the Paris Metro (whose ethnology I have not really done) I first wondered about my profession in the light of the paradoxical feeling of foreignness I experienced on returning to France. And it was thus, again, that the functions of president of the EHESS (École des Hautes Études en Sciences Sociales), exercised from 1985 to 1995, took me to several continents where I often came to reflect on the spaces I was crossing. And it was once more thus that, borrowing their terrain from some of my students, I discovered Latin America and was able to look quite closely at such phenomena as dreams and possession; this retrospectively enriched my African experiences, because, although distinct on many points of detail, they were strangely similar overall. Finally, through a ricochet effect, the interest taken in my analyses by some architects and some artists enabled me to broaden my reflections, diversify the fields of observation and multiply spaces for encounters.

This taste for the voyage is certainly personal to me, and I could probably find some reasons for it in my background and early childhood. The essential effect has been to make me particularly sensitive to what could be called the paradoxes of spatial and temporal mobility. In its luxury versions, that mobility is amplified by the accelerated expansion of means of transport. Businessmen, politicians, celebrities hurtle about the planet in all directions, like the 'starchitects' whose signatures adorn the world's highest urban pinnacles. Tourists, for their part, fly en masse (when the situation is calm there) into countries whose own nationals are running the other way as migrants, often at the risk of their lives, and whose flight is often stopped short when they are corralled into what are effectively detention camps; the lucky ones end up in the poor districts of great cities. Whether he stays within reach of the town where he lives or travels the world, the ethnologist must keep moving physically and intellectually, and ensure that his gaze is resistant to the false transparency of things, their illusory obviousness. No doubt he is merely a witness of the planet. But if he remains true to his vocation he has a chance to understand something of the changes now in the process of transforming it, while pondering the reasons that make *him* move.

For his vocation is restlessness. There is no sedentary ethnology. Residential ethnology itself is for those willing to undergo an internal ordeal of disequilibrium. The ethnologist far from home is in a peculiar situation; his usual landmarks are no longer there, and he has no others. That absence is a challenge, an experiment and an asset. It situates the ethnologist in a place, or a non-place, from which the coherence and the arbitrariness of rules can clearly be seen. Into it, perhaps with a certain perversity, he draws his 'informants', persuading them in effect to consider as cultural what they had seen before his arrival simply as natural. Ethnology is essentially critical; without that virtue, it risks becoming estranged from the illusions it is charged with bringing to light. The general anthropology which is its final form is interested in everything, but pauses over nothing. It is not relativist, and studies differences only to bypass them. In this sense it is essentially migratory.

A few ethnologists, captivated by those they were studying, have settled permanently among them. They were mistaking their profession, changing their vocation. For the ethnologist must know how to leave and get back on the road, given that he is a traveller not only in space, but in time. Perhaps a real ethnologist is led to make a journey of his own life. Back on the road, all referential places lost to sight, he will come across itinerants or wanderers, witnesses more or less aware of the change of scale affecting all the planet's inhabitants, to the benefit of some, the misfortune of others and the vertigo of all. In our world, subjected to the triple acceleration of knowledge/information, communication technologies and the market, the gap is widening by the day between the representation of a globality without borders allowing goods, people, images and messages to circulate in total freedom, and the reality of a divided, fragmented planet where the divisions denied by the ideology of the system are lodged at its very heart. Thus the 'city-world', whose networks encircle the planet and proclaim an increasingly homogeneous image of it, contrasts vividly with the harsh realities of the 'world-city' where differences and inequalities are everywhere, sometimes leading to violent confrontation.

The steady urbanization of the world, in both these senses, is the sociological and geographical truth of what we call globalization, but it is a truth infinitely more complex than that image of borderless globality which serves as an alibi for some and an illusion for others. Today we need more than ever to speak of the future in the plural, and the ethnologist who has always distrusted the definite article, especially in the singular (*the* savage, *the* primitive society), will be the first to rejoice. Neither multicultural society nor social media (heirs of the late global village), nor the consumer or service society are the last word of history, for that final word does not exist. So the ethnologist can be consoled for not being a prophet.

Nor do we know where the adventure of knowledge will take us. When we do, generic man could recognize himself in the image of God and, since to speak of generic man necessarily means taking account of the billions of individuals composing the human galaxy, monotheism and polytheism could accordingly become reconciled, or erased together. That outcome will never be known, for knowledge is unending, but we might perhaps focus on the fact that our most spectacular cities, the ones where new cathedrals of mercantile capitalism are clustered, increasingly resemble spaceships out of science fiction or the sort of buildings that man on some still-remote day will construct on other planets. As if we were already busy setting up the background scenery of our future encounters.

At a time when the planets of the solar system are beginning to be seen as mere suburbs of the Earth, when scientific popularization offers us hypotheses whose language is beyond us, and which make the mysteries cobbled together by terrestrial monotheisms seem pale and tame by comparison, Nature is no longer either a refuge or a help, but a challenge. A challenge to human societies to give priority to the only thing that can give them mastery of the future, and the only thing that can give meaning to a singular individual human life by universalizing it: the quest for the true, the real. Perhaps it is at the centre of the most vertiginous ambitions of science that the secret of the innermost wisdom of individuals is to be found. And perhaps it is awareness of the common future that can give each individual the strength to live through this shifting present which we call the future.